Saved Leader's Guide

Saved Leader's Guide

Experiencing the Promise of the Book of Acts

Nancy Guthrie

CROSSWAY®

WHEATON, ILLINOIS

Library of Congress Cataloging-in-Publication Data

Names: Guthrie, Nancy, author.
Title: Saved leader's guide : experiencing the promise of the Book of Acts / Nancy Guthrie.
Description: Wheaton, Illinois : Crossway, 2024. | Includes bibliographical references.
Identifiers: LCCN 2023053504 (print) | LCCN 2023053505 (ebook) | ISBN 9781433594915 (trade paperback) | ISBN 9781433594922 (pdf) | ISBN 9781433594939 (epub)
Subjects: LCSH: Bible. Acts—Commentaries. | Christian leadership. | Bible study.
Classification: LCC BS2625.53 .G89 2024 (print) | LCC BS2625.53 (ebook) | DDC 226.607—dc23/
  eng/20240301
LC record available at https://lccn.loc.gov/2023053504
LC ebook record available at https://lccn.loc.gov/2023053505

BP			33	32	31	30	29	28	27	26	25	24
15	14	13	12	11	10	9	8	7	6	5	4	3	2	1

Contents

Author's Note

THIS LEADER'S GUIDE HAS BEEN prepared to equip you to plan and lead a group study of the book of Acts using the book or video series *Saved: Experiencing the Power of the Book of Acts*. Acts is the longest book in the New Testament. So it is a lot to cover! I'm hoping that what Amy Kannel and I have put together in this leader's guide will really help you at every step.

This study covers the twenty-eight chapters of Acts in eighteen sessions—an introductory session plus seventeen sessions on the entire text of the book. I have sought to keep the chapters and video teaching sessions relatively short in hopes that it will not be overwhelming. But it will require perseverance to work through all eighteen sessions together.

We've tried to make the elements of this study as flexible as possible to accommodate the various ways groups will use them. The personal Bible study questions are designed to get participants into the text themselves, becoming familiar with the flow of events while also beginning to grapple with the "whys" underneath the text. While there is usually one personal application question in each personal Bible study lesson, application is mostly reserved for the teaching chapter or video and the group discussion. By using all three elements (personal Bible study + book or video + group discussion questions), we hope your group members will make discoveries in the word, grow in their understanding of the bigger picture, and have meaningful times together discussing what you're learning and how you want it to shape you.

It is likely that participants in your study will be familiar with the story of Pentecost in Acts 1–2 and with some of the other stories, such as Ananias and Sapphira (yikes!), Peter's vision of the animals on a sheet, Paul and Silas singing in prison, and perhaps the shipwreck at the end. We want to know and understand those stories. But we want more than that from our study of Acts. We want to gain a clearer sense of how the events of this book fit into the outworking of God's salvation plan. We want to see how he is at work by his Spirit through his word to build his kingdom, to gather a people for himself, a bride for his Son, made up of Jews and Gentiles.

As I have worked on this study, I've found that my understanding of Acts has made a difference in how I read the rest of the New Testament Epistles. I notice characters and situations in the Epistles that I first met or learned about in Acts. When I read the letters to the churches in Philippi, Corinth, Ephesus, or Thessalonica, I read them in light of the history of Paul's initial work in bringing the gospel to those cities. When I read Paul's commendations at the ends of some of his letters, I recognize the names of people who traveled with him and supported him in the events presented in Acts. This has made the people and events in Acts and the Epistles so much more connected and real to me. It has given me more of a sense of what it was like to follow Jesus in these early days after the ascension of Christ—the wonder as well as the costliness of it. It has made me examine myself, looking for a similar commitment to spreading the gospel and a similar willingness to suffer for the name of Jesus.

When we read Acts, we're not reading ancient history that is disconnected from us in the here and now. Rather, we're reading family history. We're reading the story of how our brothers and sisters first began to take the gospel from Jerusalem, to Judea and Samaria, and to the end of the earth. And we're seeing what it cost them. I pray that as you meet the people in this book, they will become real to you and beloved by you. I pray that you'll have a greater sense of how the risen and enthroned Lord Jesus is directing the spread of his gospel from heaven, not only during the time period covered in Acts, but today. And I pray you'll become more aware of and grateful for the Holy Spirit, who empowers his people to boldly spread that gospel. I pray that this study of Acts will cause you to understand more fully and cherish more fondly the salvation that God is accomplishing in his world and in our lives.

Nancy Guthrie

Planning Your Study

AS A LEADER, YOU HAVE THE FREEDOM to choose how to use these resources in a way that will work best for your group. Below we've sought to outline some considerations as you decide on the homework to assign, the length of your study, and how you'll divide up your time together.

How to Structure Your Study

This study can be done with or without the video version of the teaching. The content of the videos is the same as the chapters in the book.

For your first meeting, I suggest that you either have participants read the introduction in the book in advance, read the introduction aloud in your gathering, cover its content in your own words, or watch the introduction video, and then work through the discussion questions provided for the introduction session. You might also use this time to talk about how your time will be structured and clarify expectations. Your participants can then work on the personal Bible study for chapter 1 on their own prior to the next gathering.

If participants are working on the personal Bible study on their own, *we generally do not recommend that you plan to spend your time together going over all the personal Bible study questions.* These questions are invaluable for laying a foundation of understanding and helping participants immerse themselves in Scripture prior to reading the chapter or watching the video, but they do not always lend themselves very well to group discussion because they often generate simply factual responses.

You will want to use the discussion questions as your primary source for generating thoughtful discussion. These questions are designed to lead you from the text of the Bible and the chapter or video presentation into real life, deepening your understanding of the text and its implications, and making personal applications. Questions from the personal Bible study are occasionally brought into the discussion questions where we think discussing them would be helpful.

Note: If you assign the personal Bible study as homework and have someone in your group who repeatedly does not complete it, you might see if she would be interested in meeting for lunch, coffee, or a study session to work through it together. Perhaps there is an intimidation or frustration factor that you can help with.

Using Your Group Time

Following are just two examples of how you might plan your group time together based on how long you meet, whether you're using the book or the video, and whether you want to work through the personal Bible study individually or as a group. Of course, these examples are not exhaustive, but we hope they will give you ideas as you plan your study in a way that will work best for your group.

If you are using the teaching videos in this series, you will find that they vary slightly but generally last 30–45 minutes.

*Example 1: Sixty minutes using book only, with
participants reading the chapter in between gatherings:*

   5 minutes: Welcome and prayer.

15 minutes: Leader talks through main points of chapter,
             asking participants to share parts of the chapter
             that were significant.

35 minutes: Work through discussion questions.

   5 minutes: Prayer of response to material, close.

Example 2: Ninety minutes using video:

   5 minutes: Welcome, get settled, announcements.

35 minutes: Watch video teaching.

35 minutes: Discussion using the discussion questions.

10 minutes: End with various participants praying in response
             to what has been presented and discussed. Each
             session of the discussion questions ends with
             an invitation to pray through what has been
             presented in the passage.

Using the Personal Bible Study Questions

Work through questions on your own first. We all know that it
can be a challenge to resist looking for the answers to a crossword
puzzle in the back of the book. As the leader, it may likewise be
a challenge for you to resist using this resource when you work
through these questions for the first time. *We strongly urge you to
use a blank copy of the personal Bible study and complete the questions
on your own first, just like your fellow group members, without reading
the possible answers in this leader's guide until after you've completed
it on your own.* After working through the questions yourself, you

can look over the leader's guide and add notes to your own answers as desired in preparation for the group discussion.

The possible answers to the personal Bible study questions found in this leader's guide are provided to assist you and other small-group leaders in facilitating discussion and dealing with difficult questions. *This guide should never be provided to group members.* Think of it as a reference tool. If you choose to discuss the answers to the personal Bible study questions when you gather, be sure to avoid referring to what is provided in this leader's guide as the source of the "right" or "best" answer.

The personal Bible study is much less focused on personal application and much more about laying scriptural groundwork. It doesn't tie up loose ends (we hope the book chapter or the video will help to clarify any confusing concepts) and doesn't always make direct application. Its primary purpose is to get participants into God's word to see for themselves what it says and begin thinking about what it means.

Depending on the Bible study experience, maturity level, or personalities of the people in your group, some may tend to get impatient with these "What does this passage say?" questions and want to rush to application: "What does this have to do with my life?" Often in our instant-gratification culture, women want to put in a few minutes of Bible reading and come away with a feel-good bit of encouragement or a clear to-do list. They're seeking a quick "How does this apply to me?" takeaway.

Applying the Bible to our lives is essential! But the appropriate application is not always immediately clear. It's good for us to press in and think deeply to gain clarity about what the text meant to the original audience (them/then) before we bring it into our own context (us/now). If we don't spend much time on the "So what?" question in the personal Bible study, that doesn't mean it won't be addressed at all. Rather, we believe that the application will be deeper and more powerful (and more faithful to the Scriptures) when we get there if we invest the time to think carefully and understand what God's word says first. Each chapter in the book and each video presentation will present some ideas for application. And much of the discussion guide focuses on getting practical and living out the truths presented. We should keep in mind, however, that the most important impact of the lessons may be less about "what I'm supposed to do" or "how I'm supposed to change" and more about leading us to wonder and worship in light of the magnificence of God's salvation plan and the generosity of "Everyone who calls on the name of the Lord shall be saved" (Acts 2:21).

How Long Should It Take to Complete the Personal Bible Study Questions?

There is no set time frame. We all approach this differently. Some participants love to linger, think through, look up, and write out. Others simply look for the answers and make short notations. If you're asked about the time commitment, we suggest you say that it takes as much time as they choose to invest in it. Some lessons include more passages to look up than others, but we would expect that you could read the Scriptures and complete the questions in thirty to sixty minutes. Certainly participants may have more time available some weeks than others, but we all know that we get more out of study the more we put into it. As the leader, keep in mind that the depth of thought given to the lesson is not necessarily reflected in the length of answers written on the page or the time spent according to the clock.

What is most important is not how much time it takes, but that each participant plan a time to work through the personal Bible study and keep that appointment. In fact, on the first week, you might go around the circle and ask each group member to share with the group when she intends to work on the personal Bible study in the coming week. This encourages planning and establishes some accountability, as well as providing ideas to others in the group for when they might make time for study. You might ask those who have done similar studies if they prefer to do it in one sitting or to break it up over several days.

It will be wise for you to affirm at the start why we are doing any of this: because we want to know Christ through his word. This is not like the busywork we did in school. This is the pursuit of relationship with Christ, which comes primarily as we open up God's word to hear him speak to us as we read it, think it through for ourselves, chew on it, discuss it, and pray through it. It is both elements—the personal Bible study and the teaching (either book or video)—that prepare participants to take part in the group discussion.

Using the Group Discussion Questions

You will find a copy of the discussion questions for each session beginning on page 203 of this leader's guide. You may copy and hand out these questions to your group members if you would like, though you don't have to.

The discussion questions don't always lend themselves to simple answers; they invite participants to interact with the themes and challenges of each passage and consider how we are called to live in light of these truths. You will want to spend some time going over the questions on your own prior to your group time. Looking over the notes we've provided will give you a sense of the types of conversations we're hoping to provoke. But we hope you'll view this guide as a resource, not as a script. You might choose to add an opening question that will help participants warm up, or you might be selective about which questions you think will be most effective with your group and fit in your time frame. You may also want to encourage participants to share something that was meaningful or challenging to them from the personal Bible study, the book chapter, or the video presentation, determining ahead of time at what point in the discussion you will invite those comments.

We strongly urge you not to read answers from this leader's guide, as this creates a "right answer" environment rather than a genuine discussion among equal participants. Instead, we suggest you make some notes from the leader's guide onto your copy of the discussion questions and bring them in where needed, esteeming the input of your group. Their contributions may be different from what we've provided—and even more insightful!

Ideas and Resources for Discussion Group Facilitators

THANK YOU FOR YOUR WILLINGNESS to lead a group through this study of Acts! We pray that your extra investment of time and effort in preparation will not only equip you to lead effectively but will also fill you with wonder and worship of the God who is working out his salvation purposes in history.

Your Goal as Discussion Leader

What is your role as a discussion leader? We suggest you make it your goal to draw out the members of your group and guide them through a time of open and authentic discussion of the biblical truths presented in the text of Scripture and in the book or video. As you seek to clarify challenging concepts, solidify the group's grasp of the truths presented, and apply those truths to real life, work to create an environment that is safe for personal struggle, difficult questions, discovery, and even ambiguity.

Sometimes we are anxious about leading or reluctant to lead because we know we don't have all the answers. We're afraid someone will ask a question we can't answer or take the discussion in a direction we can't handle. Don't allow yourself to be intimidated by the false expectation that if you step up to facilitate the discussion, you must have all the "right" answers.

Too often when people discuss the Bible, someone in the group (often the leader) feels he or she must sum up every part of the discussion with the "right" answer. As you lead your group, avoid the compulsion to come quickly to the "right" answer to every question. Don't be afraid to let some questions hang for a while. Allow members to struggle with the issues involved in the series of questions. Keep asking for the input of other participants who may be reluctant talkers.

There's nothing wrong with admitting that you don't know something or don't fully understand something. Perhaps you need to study it more, or you want to invite someone on the pastoral staff of your church to help answer the question. Determine to lead your group as a fellow learner, not as an all-knowing expert. Expect God to use his word not only in the lives of your group members, but in your life as well!

While you do not want to dominate the group, you do want to lead effectively. It's your job to create an atmosphere that fosters meaningful discussion. As the leader, you set the tone for authenticity and openness. Set an example of being a good listener and giving short answers so that others can talk. Being an effective leader also means that it is up to you to draw reluctant talkers into the conversation and to redirect the conversation when it has gone off track. Few people want to be part of a group that is inflexible, restrictive, or rules oriented, but they do want to be part of a group that is organized and purposeful, in which expectations are unapologetically communicated and guidelines are respected. On the following pages, we've provided some suggestions for dealing with issues that commonly arise in small-group studies. We hope they will be helpful to you in leading well.

Using Your Time Effectively

As the leader, it's your responsibility to direct how the time for group discussion is used. While some participants may be very casual about this, others in your group will be very aware of the time and become frustrated when they feel their valuable time is being wasted. Several issues can have a significant impact on effectively using the time allotted for small-group discussion:

Getting Started

So often we run out of time because we are slow to get started. We are waiting for latecomers or chatting or enjoying some food together, and we simply let the time get away from us. All groups develop a culture, and members learn whether the group will really start on time or not. They will adjust their sense of urgency regarding arrival time accordingly.

Certainly you need to allow some time for participants to greet each other and to share their lives with each other, but you will want to decide how long that will last and give the group a firm start time for the discussion. If you establish a culture of starting on time regardless of whether everyone in the group has arrived, not allowing latecomers to interrupt your discussion when they arrive, you may likely find that group members become more punctual.

At the beginning of the study, you may also want to ask that any members who arrive late simply join the group and enter the discussion as unobtrusively as possible. When we stop the discussion while everyone greets the late arrival, perhaps hearing the story of what caused the lateness, it can be challenging to get started again.

You as the leader will need to manage this area with an appropriate blend of firmness and grace.

Prayer Requests

Many times we want our small-group discussion times to include sharing prayer requests, which can be a meaningful way of sharing our lives together and exercising our trust and relationship with God. But we also know that sometimes sharing requests can turn into long stories and lengthy discussions as other members offer advice or input.

If the use of time for prayer requests is a concern for your group, one way to handle this is to provide notecards for people to write down their requests. These cards can be shared at the end, or members can simply swap cards with each other. Alternatively, you may want to determine a time to bring your discussion to a close that will allow space at the end for sharing requests, praying together over those requests, and *praying through the truths presented in the lesson.*

And that is key—that your prayer time include praying through the truths presented, not solely praying over situations in the lives of participants. When we read and study God's word, we don't want it to be a one-way conversation. We want to respond to it in prayer. Rather than listening to him speak to us and then only talking to him about what we think is important, we should pray through the implications of what we've studied as an important way to respond to what he has said.

Getting Stuck Along the Way

It's easy to give too much time to questions at the beginning and end up running out of time to cover everything. We strongly suggest you go over the discussion questions in advance to determine how you will use the time. Mark the key questions you must get to. You may want to make a note beside each question that you want to be sure to include, indicating an estimate of how much time you want to give for discussing that question, and then watch your clock along the way to keep on track. As you do, however, don't be so rigidly tied to the clock that you rush the group along when rich discussion is developing. Perhaps some members found a different question particularly compelling, and a discussion that stays on topic but goes in a different direction than the one you planned can still be worthwhile and helpful.

Keeping the Focus on God's Word

People come to a Bible study for many reasons, from many situations and struggles, with varying levels of knowledge of and interest in the Bible. Sometimes a group can easily shift from a Bible study into more of a personal support group. Finding that balance between biblical study and relational connection is a challenge for every small-group leader.

Some group leaders feel that when a group member arrives with a significant struggle or sorrow, the leader must set the study aside to listen and care for that hurting person. In some situations, perhaps this is the best thing to do, but we must also remember that the word of God speaks into every need and situation in our lives. It heals; it gives perspective; it instructs, convicts, restores, and renews. Don't assume that the advice and input of group members has more power than your discussion of the truths of God's word to help that hurting person.

Keep in mind that while some participants may come more for the fellowship and sharing of their lives with each other, other participants are hungry to feast on biblical teaching and discussion of God's word. If, over time, these participants find that the word is often set aside or given short shrift, they may look for somewhere else to study God's word with others.

Ending on Time

Just as starting promptly demonstrates that participants' time is valuable, concluding your study on time also shows respect for your participants. Be sure to wrap things up at the agreed-upon time, recognizing that they have other commitments and plans after your study. That way those who want to stay and chat can linger, but those who need to leave won't have to slip out one by one, or be unable to focus on the discussion because of the distraction of needing to be somewhere else.

Guiding the Discussion and Addressing Challenges

Sharing of Opinion without Regard to God's Word

It is only natural that group members will often begin their input in the discussion with the words, "Well, I think . . ." And in fact, some of the questions are phrased in a "What do you think" manner. This is purposeful, not only to get people thinking, but also to emphasize that there isn't necessarily a right or wrong answer.

But we also want to cultivate a respect for the authority of Scripture in our discussions. Though this is not a welcome perspective in our culture, every opinion does not have equal value or weight with every other opinion. The revealed truth of God's word must carry the greatest weight in our discussions. While you don't want to embarrass someone in the group setting who states something that is clearly unscriptural, it may be a good idea to gently challenge a questionable opinion with something like, "That's interesting.

I wonder how you would support that from Scripture?" Or you might want to find a time outside the group setting to discuss the issue, using biblical support to gently challenge error.

The Discussion Gets Lively but Off Track

Sometimes the discussion quickly gets away from the original question and onto an interesting but not directly related topic. When this happens, it may be wise to state the obvious and then turn the focus back to the content at hand by saying something like, "We could certainly talk a long time about _____, but we have so much important material to discuss in our lesson this week, so let's get back to that." If the first person to answer says something that seems far from the main point, you might say, "That's interesting. How do you see that connecting to [restate the question/topic]?" If you haven't gotten to some of the key truth involved in the question, go back and ask the original question again, perhaps adding, "Did anyone see it differently or have another idea?"

Group Members Are Quiet and Slow to Respond

For a leader to be effective, it's essential for her to become comfortable with silence. Some people are slow to warm up or take longer to formulate their thoughts. Others are eager to participate but don't want to appear to be know-it-alls or dominate the discussion time. Some fear having the "wrong" answer or revealing their biblical illiteracy, especially if they are surrounded by people they perceive to have more biblical knowledge than they do. Resist the temptation to fill the silence by continuing to explain the question or jumping in with your own thoughts. Waiting quietly allows people more space to contribute. One way to deal with an awkward silence is to make a joke about the silence without coming across as chiding your group. Humor is a great way to defuse discomfort. One leader we know sometimes says, "I can wait you out!"

Be wise and careful about putting people on the spot, but where it seems appropriate, don't be afraid to call on specific people to answer questions. Some people simply don't like to answer a question unless they're invited to do so, and often these people have very thoughtful answers that will benefit the group. You might turn to the reluctant participant and say, "What do you think about that, Joan?" or, "Is that how you see it, Kim?"

Work to develop a habit of affirming the answers and willingness of those who share in your group. Set the example of being a responsive and attentive listener. Make a point of commenting on participants' input as insightful, something you've never thought of before, or personally helpful to you. Resist the temptation to sum up or add to every answer given, though it may be helpful to restate an answer if you can help to clarify something that someone is struggling to articulate. You can also generate genuine give-and-take by asking a follow-up question to someone's statement or by asking that person to tell you more about what she has said. Make sure you are focusing on the person who is sharing rather than on what you will say next.

One Person Dominates the Discussion

Almost every group has at least one person who tends to be quick to answer every question or dominate the discussion. When this pattern develops, you might begin the next question by saying, "I'd love to hear from someone who has not shared yet today." Or you might direct your next question specifically to another group member.

Sometimes, when a participant is speaking too long, you serve the group and the discussion by discreetly interrupting, perhaps saying something like, "What you're saying is helpful! I'd love to hear someone else's thoughts." Or you could summarize what she has said in a concise statement and use it as a transition to the next question. Another method is to jump in with a question such as, "What verse or phrase helped you to see that?" Remember, the other group members want and need you to take charge in this situation to keep the discussion moving and fruitful for everyone.

If the problem persists, you may need to pull your eager participant aside at some point. Invite her to be your ally in bringing more people into the discussion. She may not even realize that she is dominating. Tell her that you really appreciate her insights and want to create an atmosphere in the group in which everyone is sharing. Suggest that she could choose two or three of the questions that she really wants to answer and refrain from answering questions less important to her, so that others in the group might be more able and willing to participate.

Participants Habitually Do Not Complete the Homework

Everyone has times when life circumstances make it difficult to complete the lesson. But when group members are consistently not completing the personal Bible study or reading the chapter (if using the book only), it is a problem. Lack of preparation leaves little foundation for group discussion.

At the beginning of your time together in the first session, emphasize the importance of completing the assignments. Reiterate this the second time you meet. Without being rigid or lacking in grace, call participants to follow through on their commitment to the study rather than giving them an easy out every time. As humans we all need accountability. But sometimes in Bible study groups, we are so afraid of offending participants that we do not fulfill our role as leaders by encouraging faithfulness, punctuality, and full participation. If someone struggles to get the lessons done, you might:

- Suggest that rather than merely hoping to find some time during the week, she should make an appointment for a specific time on her calendar to complete the lesson and commit to keeping the appointment, just like she would for a lunch date with a friend or a doctor's appointment.

- Ask how she tends to use Sunday, the Lord's Day. Could she find an hour during that day to spend in God's word?

- Explore the possibility of her setting a time during the week to meet in person or by phone with another group member to work through the material together.

If she continues to be unable to complete the work, don't worry about it if it does not adversely affect the rest of the group. We cannot always know what another person's life is like, and if the best she can do is get there, that may be enough.

Disagreement with What Is Being Taught

Sometimes seeing things a little differently can be very productive in a group discussion. We learn from each other as we discover and discuss the differences or nuances in how we see things. Many topics in this study allow for a breadth of perspectives, and some topics challenge what may be dearly held views. Having to reconsider your own convictions or assumptions in light of others' perspectives is a difficult but valuable practice that can help everyone to grow.

Give each other grace and space to land in different places or agree to disagree.

What is not welcome in the group is an argumentative spirit or combative approach to what is being presented. If areas of disagreement come up that cannot be productively resolved in the group, you could respond with, "I appreciate your perspective on that. We need to move on in our discussion, but if you're interested, we could get together or meet with Pastor _____ and talk through this more. I'm sure we both have more to learn about this."

Because we are humans dealing with other humans, we will have areas of disagreement. Our different experiences and preferences will lead us to different conclusions. But that doesn't mean that we cannot have unity as we seek to submit ourselves to God's word. Make this—and every other aspect of the study—a matter of prayer as you prepare to lead your group.

A Final Note of Encouragement

The best news about leading a Bible study group is that God always equips us to do what he calls us to do. Ask God to give you the wisdom to work through whatever may come up in your small group. Ask him for insight into the personalities of the people in your group and the backgrounds that have made them who they are and shaped their perspectives about the Scriptures. Ask God to fill your heart with love for your group members as you lead them through this study of his word. And join us in praying that as you and your group members see how the enthroned Lord Jesus is at work through his Spirit to advance his glorious plan of salvation, you will be amazed by his power and eager to participate in the spread of his gospel.

PERSONAL BIBLE STUDY AND DISCUSSION QUESTIONS WITH POSSIBLE ANSWERS

Introduction

Acts of the Apostles?

Personal Bible Study

There is no personal Bible study to be completed prior to the introductory session.

Discussion Questions

1. Some of us may have studied Acts before, while others of us may be completely new to it. When you think about the book of Acts (the largest book of the New Testament), what do you already know—or think you know—about it?

   Personal response.

2. As we trace the progress of the gospel in Acts, it will be helpful for us to consult various maps of the known world in the first century. Take a moment to explore your Bible. What map(s) do you find that might prove helpful during this study?

   Personal response.

3. Nancy talked about the personal Bible study questions she has prepared to help us to get into the text of Acts. Are you planning to work through the personal Bible study prior to each session? Where can you make time in your schedule for completing it?

Personal response.

4. Nancy presented various possible titles for the book of Acts: Acts of the Apostles, Acts of the Holy Spirit, Acts of the Preached Word, and Acts of the Enthroned Lord Jesus. How are each of these "actors" significant in accomplishing the salvation of God?

The apostles are the vessels through whom God carries out his plan. May we never overlook how incredible it is that God chooses to work through humans—he doesn't need us, but he grants us the privilege and joy of participating in his work.

The Holy Spirit fills believers, empowering them to proclaim the gospel and perform signs and wonders. The Spirit grants people repentance and draws them to believe in Jesus.

The preached word is the tool the apostles use to draw people to God. It almost seems to take on an identity of its own in Acts, repeatedly described as spreading, increasing, and multiplying.

And through the apostles, the Spirit, and the word, the enthroned Lord Jesus is at work. He is still active from heaven, providing for his disciples and adding believers to his church.

5. The central aim of Acts is to assure us that the Lord Jesus is at work by his Spirit, through the word of God preached and

written by the apostles, to save a vast people for himself. Why might Luke's original audience have needed that assurance? Why might we need that assurance today?

Immediately after Jesus's ascension, it would be natural to wish Jesus were still among you. "How amazing it must have been for those who got to see him and walk with him!" you might think. "Why couldn't he have stayed? Look at all we missed out on!" And two thousand years later, isn't it easy for us to feel the same? It seems like following him would be so much easier if he were physically present with us. But Luke writes to assure them then, as well as us now, that even though Jesus is not visible, he is no less active in our lives and in the world around us. He is in heaven, but he is not far off or disinterested. He loves and cares for us. He is committed to building his church. Knowing that he is with us and at work through us gives us confidence to join him in his work.

6. Salvation is past, present, and future, so we can rightly say, "I have been saved; I am being saved; I will be saved." How does this challenge your thinking about what it means to be "saved"? What are we being saved from in each of these three aspects of salvation?

Initially, at the point of regeneration, our sins are forgiven—entirely and completely. We have been delivered from sin's penalty. Through faith, we are reckoned to be righteous—as righteous as Christ is. Then as we learn to walk with Christ in this life, we are gradually being delivered from sin's power. Ultimately, in heaven, we will be delivered from sin's presence.

We could also call this the three stages of salvation: justification, sanctification, and glorification.

7. What do you personally hope to get out of this study of Acts?

Personal response.

Let's close by praying that God will impress upon us the wonders of his salvation plan for his people as we work our way through this study of Acts.

Lesson 1

You Will Be My Witnesses

ACTS 1:1–26

Personal Bible Study

1. Read Acts 1:1–3, which serves as a summary of what Luke wrote in the Gospel of Luke and what he is going to write in this first chapter of Acts. When you read that Jesus spent forty days "speaking about the kingdom of God" with the apostles, what kinds of things do you think he might have discussed? (You might also want to read Luke 24:44–48, which provides another statement about what Jesus taught the apostles, or use your concordance to find other passages that refer to the kingdom.)

Ever since the beginning of Luke, which we could think of as part 1 of a two-part book (Luke-Acts), Luke has connected Jesus and his kingdom to the promises made to King David. The Lord promised David a son who would sit on his throne and rule over a kingdom that would last forever (2 Sam. 7:12–16; Luke 1:31–33). So Jesus likely helped the disciples connect all the Old Testament promises of a king and a kingdom of justice and righteousness to himself and his kingdom.

We can infer from the Gospels that Jesus likely spoke to them about the nature of the kingdom, perhaps reminding them of his parables (Luke 13:18–30, for example) and how he showed signs of the kingdom in his miracles (see Matt. 9:35). Perhaps he reminded them of the kingdom values he preached in Luke 6:17–49.

Throughout his ministry on earth, Jesus repeatedly spoke of the many ways his kingdom is not like kingdoms of the world. So perhaps he continued to differentiate his kingdom from worldly kingdoms. Perhaps he reminded them of who could and could not be a part of his kingdom (Luke 6:20; 9:62; 13:29; 18:15–17, 24). He might have reiterated to them how he had taught them to pray, "Your kingdom come" (Luke 11:2), instructing them that they should continue to pray for it to come in all its glorious fullness.

He may have also reminded them of the parable he had told in response to their expectation that "the kingdom of God was to appear immediately" (Luke 19:11–27). This would have encouraged them to steward what he entrusted to them as they awaited his return.

And perhaps he emphasized the "all nations" aspect of the kingdom, helping them see how God's plan all along was to include the Gentiles. Perhaps he took them to Isaiah 49 to explain that it was "too light a thing" that he as servant of

*the Lord should raise up and preserve only the tribes of Jacob
but rather that his intent was and is to make them "a light
for the nations, that my salvation may reach to the end of
the earth" (Isa. 49:6).*

2. Read Acts 1:4. Jesus tells the disciples to wait for "the promise
   of the Father." What do the following verses reveal about this
   promise?

   Isaiah 32:14–15: *The Spirit will be poured out on God's people,
   transforming them from being like wilderness to a fruitful field.*

   Isaiah 44:3: *The Spirit will be poured out on Israel's offspring.*

   Joel 2:28–29: *The Spirit will be poured out on all flesh so that
   all of God's people will prophesy.*

3. Read Acts 1:6–7. The disciples' question, "Lord, will you at
   this time restore the kingdom to Israel?" could be understood
   a number of ways. How would the following passages have
   shaped the disciples' expectations of "restoration"?

   Isaiah 49:5–6: *Restoration means bringing Israel back to God
   and making them a light to the nations so that his "salvation
   may reach to the end of the earth."*

   Ezekiel 37:20–28: *The tribes of the northern and southern
   kingdoms will become one nation in the land again, with one
   king over them. Idolatry will be a thing of the past. God will
   dwell with them in a covenant of peace, claiming them as his
   own and identifying himself as their God. All nations will
   know that he sanctifies them and is in their midst.*

Zechariah 2:10–11: *God will welcome Gentiles into the people of God.*

4. Read Acts 1:8, which provides a rough outline for the entire book of Acts. Consider who Jesus was speaking to. Why might this statement from Jesus have been challenging for them to grasp?

   Jesus spoke these words to twelve Galileans who had likely never traveled widely or interacted much with Gentiles. Their sense was that Jesus was a Messiah for the Jews. It probably never occurred to them that they would testify about Jesus to Gentiles, or that they would go "to the end of the earth." They probably found it hard to grasp what it would mean for the Holy Spirit to "come upon" them.

5. Read Acts 1:9–11. What details do these verses provide about the ascension and return of Christ?

   Jesus, in his human body, was lifted up from the earth. He was enveloped in a cloud. Two men in white robes stood by the disciples and spoke to them. Then men in white robes told them that Jesus was taken up into heaven and that he will return to earth in the same way.

6. Read Acts 3:19–21. What does Peter come to understand about the time of restoration?

   The time of full restoration will come when Jesus returns to earth.

7. Read Acts 1:12–20. In verse 16, Peter says that the psalms of David he is quoting (Psalms 69:25 and 109:8) are fulfilled in

Judas. How do you think Peter has been able to come to that conclusion? (See Luke 24:25–27, 44–47.)

Over the forty days Jesus spent with his disciples after his resurrection, he had opened their minds to see how the Old Testament was most profoundly about him—specifically about his suffering and glory. Perhaps in "speaking about the kingdom of God" (Acts 1:3), Jesus also showed them how to understand David's psalms as not only speaking about David's own experience but more profoundly about the experiences of his greater son, King Jesus. So where Psalm 69 speaks of the enemies of God's king experiencing the curse of desolation, Peter sees Judas, who set himself as an enemy of God in his betrayal of Jesus. And when Peter reads in Psalm 109 that the life of the wicked man who responds to the king's love with hatred should be cut short and "another take his office," Peter discerns this to be about the wicked Judas, who responded to Jesus's love with hatred.

8. Read Acts 1:21–26. What requirements do you find for the replacement apostle according to these verses? (You might also consult Acts 10:39–41.)

An apostle had to have been with Jesus throughout his three years of public ministry. He had to have been an eyewitness of the resurrected Jesus. He had to be chosen by Jesus.

9. The time the apostles spent with Jesus between his resurrection and ascension helped them to grapple with the ways the kingdom of Jesus was not what they had expected it to be. They had to make some adjustments in their understanding and expectations. Has your life, as a citizen of the kingdom

of God, been what you expected it to be? What truths from Jesus's teaching about the kingdom could help you adjust your expectations toward what Jesus has promised?

Personal response.

Discussion Questions

1. Luke begins by referring to his Gospel, which was about what Jesus "began to do and teach" (Acts 1:1). This implies that Acts is about what Jesus *continued* to do and teach after his ascension. Why is it important for us to recognize that Jesus continues to "do and teach" from his throne in heaven?

   While Jesus walked on earth, he said, "I will build my church" (Matt. 16:18)—and even though he is now in heaven, he is indeed building his church. Jesus's ministry was not limited to a few years in first-century Palestine! He actively continues to "do and teach" from his throne in heaven, and his purposes cannot be thwarted or resisted. Nothing and no one can stop his plans from coming to fruition.

   We are not building his church, though in his grace he equips and uses us to be a part of his great mission. But it is not up to us. This means we do not need to be anxious in the face of opposition, persecution, or rejection. We never need to think that we are on our own in our mission to proclaim the gospel so that people from every nation will be saved. And we need not grow discouraged when the growth is slow to come. Jesus is on his throne in heaven, ruling over every aspect of God's salvation plan, and it will come about in his way and in his timing.

2. Why is the ascension of Jesus significant? Why do you think we give so much less attention to it than to his incarnation, death, and resurrection?

The ascension of the risen and glorified (and yet still human!) Jesus assures us that Jesus is still active on behalf of his people, ruling and reigning from heaven. It also encourages us to anticipate his bodily return to this earth. In the resurrection, Jesus conquered death; in the ascension, he was exalted to the right hand of the Father. When we focus solely on what he has done for us in the past in his life, death, and resurrection, we fail to realize the implications of his ongoing lordship and what he continues to do for us. We devalue his present ministry to us and for us in heaven.

Perhaps we give less attention to his ascension because we have less of a record of his ministry from heaven than we have of his ministry on earth. But while we don't have a lot of details, the New Testament gives us some powerful examples of what Jesus's ascension to the Father's right hand means for us. In his glorified human body, Jesus has gone to heaven "as a forerunner on our behalf" (Heb. 6:20). As a result of his ascension, we have "a sure and steadfast anchor of the soul, a hope that enters into the inner place behind the curtain" (Heb. 6:19). From his place in heaven, the exalted Lord bestows gifts of repentance and forgiveness of sins (Acts 5:31). And he serves there as our mediator, interceding for us (Rom. 8:34).

3. What kinds of things do you think Jesus discussed with the apostles when he spent forty days with them "speaking about the kingdom of God" (Acts 1:3)?

Jesus likely taught his disciples how he is the King at the center of the kingdom. Luke 24:44–48 tells us that he helped them see how all of the Old Testament points to him, how the prophecies have been or will be fulfilled in him—that he is God's "yes" to all those promises (2 Cor. 1:20). He may have clarified for them why the cross was necessary, and how it was not the end but the beginning. He also probably emphasized the "all nations" aspect of the kingdom, helping them see how God's plan all along was to include the Gentiles. Perhaps he took them to Isaiah 49 to explain that it was "too light a thing" that he as servant of the Lord should raise up and preserve only the tribes of Jacob, but rather that his intent was and is to make them "a light for the nations, that my salvation may reach to the end of the earth" (Isa. 49:6).

4. How would the Old Testament prophets have shaped how the apostles thought about the restoration of Israel?

The prophets repeatedly spoke of a day when the twelve tribes of Israel, who were separated when the northern kingdom split from the southern kingdom, would be regathered and restored to God and to each other. A regathered and restored Israel would be a beacon of light beckoning the nations to stream to Mount Zion to worship the one true God (Isa. 11; 60; Ezek. 37:16–19).

From Isaiah 49:5–6, they could have understood that restoration would mean that Israel was brought back into loving relationship with God and that he would make them a light to the nations so that his "salvation may reach to the end of the earth."

From Ezekiel 37:20–28, they could have understood restoration coming as the tribes of the northern and southern kingdoms became one nation in the land again, with one king over them. Idolatry would be a thing of the past. God would dwell with them in a covenant of peace, claiming them as his own and identifying himself as their God.

From Zechariah 2:10–11, they could have understood that restoration would include God welcoming Gentiles into the people of God.

5. If you were an ordinary Israelite in the Old Testament era, why might you have longed for the day when "the promise of the Father," the indwelling of the Holy Spirit in all believers, would become a reality?

We likely take the Holy Spirit's indwelling of every believer for granted. We've never had to live as those who loved God and sought to obey his commands but did not have the Holy Spirit within them. The prophets had promised that the day would come when the Spirit would be poured out, cleansing them of idolatry and giving them a new heart for obedience (Isa. 44:3–4; Ezek. 36:25–28; Joel 2:28–29). Israelites under the old covenant must have longed for the power of the Holy Spirit to give them the "want-to" to obey God's commands. They must have longed to have the Spirit work in their minds to guide them into truth. They must have longed for the Spirit to comfort them with assurance of salvation. They must have longed for the conviction of the Holy Spirit that would prompt them to confess and forsake sin.

The Spirit's work in all believers would form them into a true community, empowering them to love and serve each other and the world around them. Surely the Old Testament Israelites who so often succumbed to idolatry, apathy toward God, and conflict with each other would have longed for the Spirit to be at work among them to enliven their fellowship with God and strengthen their community life.

6. Jesus tells the apostles that they would receive power to be his witnesses "in Jerusalem and in all Judea and Samaria, and to the end of the earth" (Acts 1:8). In what ways would they need divine power to accomplish this task?

   To be effective witnesses, the apostles would first need to understand and remember all that Jesus had taught them. This is exactly what Jesus had promised in John 14:26 that the Spirit would do for them. Additionally, these men had just recently fled in fear when Jesus was arrested and crucified. Clearly they would need supernatural power to stand firm and speak boldly in the face of persecution and opposition. They would also need divine power to overcome their natural prejudice against non-Jews.

7. Can the statement "You will be my witnesses" be applied directly to us today? Why or why not?

   It does apply to us today, but only derivatively, as we hold fast to the apostles' foundational gospel witness and build on that apostolic foundation (Eph. 2:20). Our calling is to proclaim what they have recorded for us in the New Testament. It is also important to recognize that, for most of us, our home base for missionary activity is not Jerusalem. Instead, we are part of "the end of the earth" reached by the gospel in the period beyond its foundational spread.

8. Nancy suggests that instead of thinking of ourselves as "witnesses," we should think of ourselves as "proclaimers." What is the difference? How might this distinction impact how we approach our mission?

    We can never be "witnesses" to Christ in the sense that the apostles were, as eyewitnesses to the resurrected Christ. And our calling isn't really to give a testimony about our own experience. That can often be a valuable part of our conversations about Christ, but it is not the focus of our message. Our calling is to proclaim the objective truth that the apostolic witnesses have recorded for us in the Gospels and Epistles about the Lord Jesus Christ. This should shape (and perhaps constrain) the content of our message. If our message is not drawn from, or does not conform faithfully to, what the apostles have recorded for us, we are not doing true gospel ministry.

9. Though we are proclaimers rather than witnesses, we need the same divine power these eyewitnesses needed to accomplish their task. And that power is available to us! In what ways do we need the Holy Spirit's power to accomplish our task?

    We need the Spirit to enlighten the eyes of our hearts (Eph. 1:18) so that we understand the word that testifies to him. We need him to convict us of sin and purify us from all unrighteousness (1 John 1:9) so that we have integrity as we proclaim truth. We need his power to communicate clearly and boldly.

We need him to give us courage in the face of opposition and wisdom to guide our steps.

Let's close by praying for each other to receive divine power for the task of proclaiming what the apostles have handed down to us.

Lesson 2

I Will Pour Out My Spirit

ACTS 2:1–47

Personal Bible Study

1. Read Acts 2:1. The events of this chapter take place on "the day of Pentecost" (2:1), one of numerous Old Testament feasts. To see the significance of this, it's helpful to review some other feasts and how they were brought to ultimate fulfillment in Jesus Christ. The original Passover recalled the sacrifice of the lambs in Egypt (Ex. 12), but it pointed forward to Jesus, who was sacrificed as the Lamb of God on Passover (Luke 22:7). On the first day after the Sabbath of Passover week was the Feast of Firstfruits (Lev. 23:9–11), in which Israelites offered the first of their harvest to God. And three days after his death, Jesus rose from the grave as the "firstfruits of those who have fallen asleep" (1 Cor. 15:20–23).

Then seven weeks after the Feast of Firstfruits came the Feast of Weeks, also called the Feast of Harvest (Ex. 23:16) or

Pentecost, which celebrated the completion or fullness of the harvest. And what we read about in Acts 2 takes place seven weeks after Jesus's resurrection, on Pentecost. Skip ahead to Acts 2:41. What kind of harvest is celebrated on this day of Pentecost?

On this Pentecost there is a great harvest of souls gathered in to Christ, the beginning of an even greater harvest of both Jews and Gentiles.

2. Read Acts 2:2–4. The 120 believers gathered in the room hear a sound "like a mighty rushing wind" and see "divided tongues as of fire." Numerous times throughout Old Testament history there was wind or fire as heavenly and earthly realms came together. What examples do you find in the following verses?

Exodus 3:2: *God spoke to Moses from a burning bush.*

Exodus 14:21: *Moses stretched out his hand over the sea, and the Lord drove the sea back by a strong east wind so the Israelites could cross on dry land.*

Exodus 19:18: *The Lord descended on Mount Sinai in fire.*

Job 38:1: *The Lord answered Job out of the whirlwind.*

Ezekiel 1:4: *The glory of God appeared to Ezekiel as fire and brightness that arrived on a stormy wind.*

Other examples include Genesis 8:1; 15:17–18; Exodus 3:2; 10:13, 19; 13:21; 14:21; 19:18; 40:38; Numbers 11:31; 16:35; 1 Kings 18:38; 2 Chronicles 7:1; Job 38:1; Isaiah 6:6–7; Ezekiel 1:4; Jonah 1:4; 4:8.

3. What do you think is the significance of the fire appearing as tongues in this instance?

This was a miracle of speech empowered by the Spirit. Just as fire can both cleanse and destroy, this was a message of cleansing for those who received it and judgment on those who rejected it.

4. Read Acts 2:5–13. On this map, circle all of the countries or areas from which Jews have gathered in Jerusalem for the feast of Pentecost.

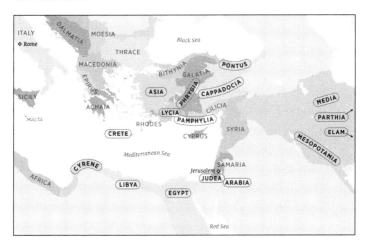

5. Read Acts 2:14–21. What do you think Peter is trying to communicate by connecting what is happening at Pentecost to Joel's prophecy? How would this be different from what a few Old Testament believers experienced to accomplish particular tasks (for example, Bezalel in Ex. 31:1–5; Balaam in Num. 24:2; Saul in 1 Sam. 10:10; and Daniel in Dan. 4:8)?

This is the pouring out of the Spirit on all flesh that had been prophesied by Joel and other prophets. Throughout the Old

Testament, the Spirit was poured out only on select individuals with special roles to play. It was a temporary outpouring rather than a permanent indwelling. Notable examples include Joseph's dream interpretation to save Egypt from famine (Gen. 41:38–39); Bezalel's gifting to design and create elements of the tabernacle (Ex. 31:1–5); various people's temporary ability to prophesy (Num. 11:25; 24:2); judges such as Gideon and Samson (Judg. 6:34; 14:6); kings such as Saul and David (1 Sam. 11:6; 16:13); and prophets and priests like Zechariah and Ezekiel (2 Chron. 24:20; Ezek. 2:2). Ordinary believers could not expect to receive the Spirit; in rare cases where they did, the outpouring was temporary.

6. The prophecy in Joel is typical of lots of Old Testament prophecy in that it foresees future events that are separated by time but speaks of them as one event. Part of Joel's prophecy is being fulfilled at Pentecost, but what still-future event is described in verses 19–21?

   The return of Christ in judgment and salvation, which is often called "the day of the Lord." On this day, all who have refused to call upon the Lord in repentance and faith will experience his terrible judgment, while all those who have called on the name of the Lord will experience his great salvation.

7. Read Acts 2:22–32. What event does Peter say David wrote about in the psalms that could not have been about David?

   The resurrection of Jesus from the dead.

8. Read Acts 2:33–36. What events does Peter say David wrote about in Psalm 110?

The ascension, heavenly enthronement, and promised return of Jesus in judgment and salvation.

9. Read Acts 2:37–41. Peter says that those who repent and are baptized will receive the gift of the Holy Spirit. How do you see the power of the Spirit at work in the following verses?

v. 36: *Certainty and the ability to trust in the lordship of Christ is a work of the Spirit.*

v. 37: *Conviction, presented as being "cut to the heart," is a work of the Spirit.*

v. 38: *Repentance is a gift (Acts 11:18). It is an act that the Holy Spirit works in us, resulting in an act that flows out of us. Baptism is a sign of the Spirit's applying the benefits of union with Christ to the believer, including the forgiveness of sins and the gift of the indwelling Holy Spirit.*

v. 39: *The Spirit is the one who calls people to himself, prompting them to call upon the name of the Lord for salvation.*

v. 41: *The Spirit makes a person open to receiving the word of Christ.*

10. Read Acts 2:42–47. The Spirit's power might seem most obvious in the "wonders and signs" the apostles were doing. But how else do you see the power of the Spirit at work in these verses?

v. 42: *The Spirit gives them a hunger for the apostles' teaching and hearts for prayer.*

v. 43: *The Spirit causes awe to come upon every soul.*

v. 45: *The Spirit makes them generous rather than self-absorbed or stingy.*

vv. 45–46: *The Spirit produces the fruit of love and joy.*

v. 47: *The Spirit grants them favor in the eyes of people who are watching them. The Spirit continues to bring people from spiritual death to spiritual life.*

11. In this passage, we see the impact of the Holy Spirit's coming on and in the first believers. In what ways has the Holy Spirit moved powerfully in your life? What are some ways you would like to see the Holy Spirit work further in your life?

Personal response.

Discussion Questions

1. The personal Bible study took you to some Old Testament examples where wind and fire were evidence of earthly and heavenly realms coming together. And perhaps you can think of some others. What kinds of things do the fire and wind accomplish or represent?

Throughout the Old Testament when God's personal presence descends to earth, it is often in the form of fire, such as the burning bush, the fire on Mount Sinai, or the pillar of fire that led the Israelites through the wilderness. Fire symbolizes God's radiant glory as an aspect of his holiness. Fire both purifies and destroys.

In the Hebrew Old Testament, the word translated "spirit" is ruach, *which can also be translated as "wind" or "breath."*

Throughout the Old Testament, God often acts to provide for and protect his people by sending a wind. He speaks out of the whirlwind. The wind blows over dry bones and brings life. The wind is an apt representation of the Spirit, as it is invisible, yet its results can be seen and felt. It is powerful, unexplainable, and beyond human control.

Old Testament examples of wind and fire include:

- *A smoking fire pot and flaming torch passed through the pieces in the covenant ceremony between God and Abram (Gen. 15).*
- *God spoke to Moses from a burning bush (Ex. 3:2).*
- *The Israelites were led by a pillar of fire at night in the wilderness (Ex. 13:21).*
- *The Lord descended on Mount Sinai in fire (Ex. 19:18).*
- *Fire came down from heaven when the glory of the Lord filled the tabernacle and later the temple in Jerusalem (Ex. 40:38; 2 Chron. 7:1).*
- *Fire came out from the Lord and consumed 250 men offering incense (Num. 16:35).*
- *Fire from God fell on Elijah's sacrifices (1 Kings 18:38).*
- *The glory of God appeared to Ezekiel as fire and brightness that arrived on a stormy wind (Ezek. 1:4).*
- *In Noah's day, God made a wind blow over the earth and the waters subsided (Gen 8:1).*
- *Moses stretched out his staff over the land of Egypt and the Lord brought an east wind that brought locusts, then a west wind that drove them away (Ex. 10:13, 19).*
- *Moses stretched out his hand over the sea and the Lord drove the sea back by a strong east wind so the Israelites could cross on dry land (Ex. 14:21).*

- *A wind from the Lord brought quail to the camp in the wilderness (Num. 11:31).*
- *The Lord answered Job out of the whirlwind (Job 38:1).*
- *The Lord hurled a great wind on the sea as Jonah sought to flee from him, then appointed a wind to make Jonah miserable in Nineveh (Jonah 1:4; 4:8).*

2. We're told that the 120 new believers in Christ are able to speak in the languages of the devout Jews and proselytes gathered in Jerusalem, telling them about "the mighty works of God" (2:11). What kinds of things do you think they might have said?

   Perhaps they began with the mighty works of deliverance and salvation in the Old Testament and used them to explain how they had all been pointing toward God's ultimate work of deliverance and salvation in the incarnation, death, and resurrection of Jesus.

3. Peter explains Pentecost as a fulfillment of Joel's prophecy that the Spirit would be poured out on all people so that they could understand and articulate the message of salvation in Christ. How was this experience of the Spirit different from what ordinary believers experienced throughout the Old Testament?

   Up to this point in history, the Spirit was poured out only on select individuals with special roles to play. It was a temporary outpouring rather than a permanent indwelling. Notable examples include Joseph's dream interpretation to save Egypt from famine (Gen. 41:38–39); Bezalel's gifting to design and create elements of the tabernacle (Ex. 31:1–5); various people's temporary ability to prophesy (Num. 11:25; 24:2); judges such as Gideon and Samson (Judg. 6:34; 14:6); kings such as Saul and David (1 Sam. 11:6; 16:13); and prophets and priests like Zechariah and Ezekiel (2 Chron. 24:20; Ezek. 2:2). Ordinary believers could not expect to receive the Spirit; in rare cases where they did, the outpouring was temporary.

4. At the end of his sermon (2:36), Peter says that based on what he has presented, they should "know for certain that God has made [Jesus] both Lord and Christ." What do you think it would have been like to be in that crowd on that day? What kinds of things might those in the crowd have been thinking?

   We know that three thousand people received the word (2:41). They were likely experiencing intense ("cut to the heart") new understanding, desire for Christ, and joy in recognizing and embracing Christ as their Savior. But many others who didn't accept what Peter presented were likely agitated or angry.

   It would have been a huge adjustment for these devout people to make the shift to embrace Jesus as Lord (the ruler over all things, to whom they must submit) and Christ (the fulfillment of all the Old Testament promises of Messiah and King).

5. Imagine being part of a new church with three thousand new believers who have come out of being devout followers of Judaism and speak many different languages. What challenges would such a church face?

*Three thousand people would all be working through adjust-
ments in their understanding of what it means to be a part of
the people of God, what he requires, and what it will mean to
worship him. There would be communication struggles, cultural
barriers, and practical issues regarding when and where they
would meet and how that time would be spent.*

6. How do we see the Spirit at work empowering this new community in Acts 2:42–47? What aspects of their life together
   do you find especially appealing?

   *The Spirit is at work making them hungry for teaching and
   fellowship. The Spirit is empowering the apostles to perform
   signs and wonders that authenticate their ministry. The Spirit
   is empowering the believers to be generous, glad, and full of
   praise to God, and he is granting them favor with the people
   around them.*

7. One way to think through the impact of Pentecost is to
   consider what would be different if it had not happened.
   How would your life be different if Jesus had ascended and
   begun to reign but had not given the Holy Spirit to dwell
   in you?

   *All believers could say that, generally speaking, without the
   Holy Spirit dwelling in us, we would have no conviction of sin,
   no power to put sin to death, no assurance of final salvation, no
   ability to understand the Bible, and no strength for perseverance in the life of faith. Encourage the members of your group
   to think about specific ways their lives are different because of
   the Holy Spirit's work in them.*

Let's pray, thanking God for the Holy Spirit and asking him to purify us with his fire, to breathe his life into us by his Spirit. Let's ask him to help us welcome the work of the Holy Spirit in our lives, even though it may push us beyond our comfort zones.

Lesson 3

In Jesus the Resurrection
from the Dead

ACTS 3:1–4:31

Personal Bible Study

1. Read through the following passages from the Old Testament
   prophets. What do they have in common?

   Then the eyes of the blind shall be opened,
   	and the ears of the deaf unstopped;
   then shall the lame man leap like a deer,
   	and the tongue of the mute sing for joy.
   For waters break forth in the wilderness,
   	and streams in the desert. (Isa. 35:5–6)

   Behold, I will bring them from the north country
   	and gather them from the farthest parts of the earth,

among them the blind and the lame,
    the pregnant woman and she who is in labor, together;
    a great company, they shall return here. (Jer. 31:8)

"Behold, at that time I will deal
    with all your oppressors.
And I will save the lame
    and gather the outcast,
and I will change their shame into praise
    and renown in all the earth.
At that time I will bring you in,
    at the time when I gather you together;
for I will make you renowned and praised
    among all the peoples of the earth,
when I restore your fortunes
    before your eyes," says the LORD. (Zeph. 3:19–20)

In that day, declares the LORD,
    I will assemble the lame
and gather those who have been driven away
    and those whom I have afflicted;
and the lame I will make the remnant,
    and those who were cast off, a strong nation;
and the LORD will reign over them in Mount Zion
    from this time forth and forevermore. (Mic. 4:6–7)

*Each of these passages talks about a future day when God will
gather, refresh, and restore his people. Common to each passage
is the promise that the lame will be healed or "saved."*

2. Read Acts 3:1–10. How does this story connect to the prophetic passages you've just read?

By the power of the risen and ascended Jesus, Peter and John heal a man who has been lame for forty years. This seems to fulfill exactly what the prophets wrote would happen in the last days. God is doing a significant and pervasive work of restoration among his people and in all of creation.

3. Read Acts 3:11–26. How would you summarize Peter's argument in this sermon?

This man has been restored to perfect health through the power of the crucified, risen, and ascended Jesus, who reigns from heaven until the time comes for restoring all things. Even those who participated in his death can get in on the grace of repentance and forgiveness and be refreshed by the indwelling Holy Spirit. This blessing that comes through Jesus is the blessing promised through Abraham.

4. Read Acts 3:11–26, in which Peter speaks about who Jesus is and what he does. What things in these verses do you think would have been especially difficult for Peter's audience to hear? What would they have found encouraging to hear?

Difficult to hear:

"Jesus whom you delivered over and denied" (v. 13).

"You denied the Holy and Righteous One" (v. 14).

"You killed the Author of life" (v. 15).

"Every soul who does not listen to that prophet shall be destroyed from the people" (v. 23).

Encouraging to hear:

"You acted in ignorance" (v. 17).

"Repent . . . , and turn back, that your sins may be blotted out" (v. 19).

". . . times of refreshing may come from the presence of the Lord, and that he may send the Christ appointed for you, Jesus" (v. 20).

"God . . . sent him to you first, to bless you, by turning every one of you from your wickedness" (v. 26).

5. Read Acts 4:1–4. How does Luke summarize what Peter and John were teaching (v. 2)? How do those who heard it respond?

   Luke sums up their message as "in Jesus the resurrection from the dead."

   The priests, the captain of the temple, and the Sadducees respond by arresting Peter and John, holding them in custody overnight. Five thousand of the people listening respond by believing Peter and John's message, placing their hope and confidence "in Jesus the resurrection from the dead."

6. Read the following Old Testament passages and note a phrase from each that would have shaped what Peter's listeners would have understood or expected regarding "the resurrection from the dead."

   Job 19:25–27: *"After my skin has been thus destroyed, yet in my flesh I shall see God."*

Isaiah 25:6–9: *"He will swallow up death forever."*

Isaiah 26:19: *"Your dead shall live; their bodies shall rise."*

Daniel 12:2: *"Many of those who sleep in the dust of the earth shall awake, some to everlasting life, and some to shame and everlasting contempt."*

7. Read Acts 4:5–12. Peter and John are interrogated by the rulers, elders, scribes, and the entire high priestly family, including Annas (the high priest) and Caiaphas. For what "crime" are they examining Peter and John? What accusations does Peter make against them?

   They are interrogating Peter and John for a good deed, not a crime. Peter accuses them of crucifying and rejecting Jesus. He also asserts that there is no salvation in the temple religious system they oversee; rather, the salvation promised by God is available only in Jesus.

8. Read Acts 4:13–22. How does this passage connect to Acts 1:8: "But you will receive power when the Holy Spirit has come upon you, and you will be my witnesses in Jerusalem and in all Judea and Samaria, and to the end of the earth"?

   The Spirit has filled these apostles with boldness. The council thinks they can keep the apostles from spreading the word of Jesus, but they cannot overcome the appointment Jesus gave the apostles to be his witnesses. The apostles can't help but be his witnesses. We also see that the news has spread "to all the inhabitants of Jerusalem," and the rulers are concerned "that it may spread no further."

9. Read Acts 4:23–31. How do the believers relate Psalm 2 to what Peter and John have just experienced? How does the quote from Psalm 2 relate to the statement in 4:28?

The believers see the opposition they're experiencing as a fulfillment of Psalm 2's description of the rulers gathering together against the Lord. In their opposition to Jesus, the Jewish religious leaders have aligned themselves with all those who have set themselves against the Lord and his anointed throughout Israel's history.

The quote from Psalm 2 shows that God foretold— indeed, he ordained—this opposition to his anointed king (Jesus) and his kingdom. While the religious leaders who called for Jesus's crucifixion and arrested the apostles acted out of their own evil jealousy and unbelief, their actions were fulfilling the eternal plan of God.

10. Peter and John are incredibly bold in speaking of Christ despite the pressures of the religious leaders. In verse 29, we read that they prayed for boldness to keep speaking the word of God. How would you rate your own boldness in speaking of Christ? What do you think it would look like for you to be bold? Are you willing to pray for boldness?

Personal response.

Discussion Questions

1. In the personal Bible study, you were asked to read passages from Isaiah, Jeremiah, Zephaniah, and Micah. What commonalities did you see? How do you think these passages relate to "in Jesus the resurrection of the dead" (Acts 4:2)?

These passages are all about the newness, healing, and whole-
ness that the Messiah will bring about when he comes. Each
specifically mentions promises of healing and salvation for
the lame. These passages, along with others in the prophets,
describe what began to come true in the first coming of Jesus
and the sending of his Spirit and will come into even greater
reality at "the resurrection of the dead"—the future day of
Christ's return.

2. How is Peter's message in Acts 3:11–21 an example to follow
   in presenting the gospel?

   Peter bases his message on the Scriptures. It is not based on
   Peter's personal experience, but on the person and work of
   Christ—his death, resurrection, present reign, and promised
   return. Peter boldly and clearly calls his listeners to repent
   so that they will have their sins forgiven and experience the
   newness of life that comes from being joined to Christ. He also
   invites them to anticipate the future new creation.

3. Take turns putting 3:19–21 in your own words. How would
   you share the substance of Peter's gospel presentation with
   those around you today?

   Turn from your rejection of Jesus and run to him so that you
   can experience his forgiveness! The refreshment that your soul
   can find through being joined to him is better than any "self-
   care" you can pursue. Jesus is in heaven now, but the time
   is coming when he will return and bring restoration and
   newness to all things, just as God promised through the Old
   Testament prophets.

4. What in Peter and John's message annoyed the priests, the captain of the temple, and the Sadducees?

They were upset because Peter and John claimed that salvation could not be found through Judaism, law-keeping, and temple worship, which was the realm in which they had power. Peter also publicly indicted them by suggesting that Psalm 118, about the builders who rejected a stone that was made the cornerstone, was really about them: they were rejecting Jesus, whom God made the cornerstone of the new temple he is building.

5 What do you think Peter is trying to communicate by quoting Psalm 2 in his prayer in Acts 4:25–28? (Consider reading the whole psalm together.) What is he saying about Jesus, and about the religious leaders who had told them not to speak? How do you think it would have helped these first believers to see their experience in light of Psalm 2?

Peter is asserting that Jesus is the Lord's anointed one as described in Psalm 2. He sees the intimidation of the religious leaders as an outworking of this ongoing conflict. The opposition they are experiencing from the religious rulers does not mean that God's plan is spinning out of control. On the contrary, Psalm 2 reflects that such opposition is simply God's plan falling into place.

Seeing their experience in light of this ongoing battle would have infused their suffering for Christ with meaning and purpose. They would also be assured of the final outcome of the conflict, strengthened in their confidence that Christ will be the ultimate victor and that they will share in his victory.

6. When you consider the background of the disciples and the way they abandoned Jesus at his arrest and crucifixion, how do you explain the boldness of Peter and John in these chapters?

After forty days of being taught by Jesus between his resurrection and ascension, Peter and John now understand the Old Testament Scriptures in a way they did not before. This gives them confidence in Jesus as the fulfillment of God's plans for salvation. They have been told by Jesus that they would be his witnesses, which gives them a sense of purpose and confidence that they are part of the outworking of God's plans for salvation being proclaimed to all nations. Most importantly, they have been filled with the Holy Spirit. Their boldness and courage reflect the Spirit's power at work in them, using their proclamation to bring people to repentance and faith.

7. What do you think are the greatest hindrances to our ability or willingness to "speak the word of God with boldness"? What do you think could happen if you were bolder?

Personal response.

Let's pray, asking for boldness to speak the word of God in specific situations or settings in our lives.

Lesson 4

You Will Not Be Able to Overthrow Them

ACTS 4:32–5:42

Personal Bible Study

1. Read Acts 4:32–36. How would you characterize what is "great" or impressive in the following verses?

   v. 33a: *Great power in testifying to the resurrection of Jesus.*

   v. 33b: *Great grace upon the believers.*

   vv. 32, 34–35: *Great generosity to other believers in need.*

2. Read Acts 5:1–11. How are Ananias and Sapphira's actions characterized in verse 3?

   Rather than being filled with the Holy Spirit, Satan has filled their hearts so that they lie to the Holy Spirit.

How are their actions characterized in verse 9?

In lying to the new community, they are lying to God himself, testing his Spirit to see if he will tolerate it or judge them for it.

Why do you think Ananias and Sapphira do this?

They are motivated by pride and fear of man rather than fear of the Lord. They care more about appearing spiritual and sacrificial than actually being so; they want to be honored and applauded by others more than they want to honor God.

3. Like Ananias and Sapphira, we too face the temptation of seeking to appear more spiritual or sacrificial than we actually are. Can you identify any specific ways or situations in which you face this temptation? What changes might you need to make in order to be more truthful with how you present your devotion to and relationship with Christ?

Personal response.

4. Read Acts 5:12–17. Why do you think the high priest and the rest of the religious council respond this way to the signs and wonders of the apostles?

The leaders of the temple have been the "go-to" source for connection to God, but now the apostles are demonstrating and exercising God's healing power. Crowds are flocking around the apostles, holding these ordinary men in high esteem, when the religious leaders had always been the ones held in high esteem by the people. They don't like being ignored or overshadowed!

And where have we heard this before? (See Matt. 27:18.)

It was out of envy that the Jews delivered Jesus up to be crucified.

5. Read Acts 5:18–32. How is the charge to the apostles from the angel who brought them out of prison the exact opposite of the charge to the apostles from the religious council?

The angel tells them to go and stand in the temple and proclaim the gospel—"all the words of this Life"—to the people. The religious council strictly charges them not to "teach in this name."

6. After the council charges them not to teach about the gospel, they immediately announce the gospel to the council. What are the key elements of the gospel, according to verses 30–32?

Jesus died and was raised from the dead, exalted to God's right hand as leader and Savior. He calls people to repent and experience forgiveness of sin and receive the Holy Spirit.

7. Read Acts 5:33–39. In verse 39, Gamaliel makes a profound statement. We are still early in the book of Acts, but from what you know about how the story will progress, how will his statement prove true in this book?

The successful spread of the gospel throughout Acts demonstrates that it is from God. The apostles' teaching does not fail, because it does not originate with them. It is unstoppable, despite repeated efforts to persecute and murder those who proclaim it.

8. Read Acts 5:40–42. Notice what they are instructed to do and what they actually do. What do you think generates the joy and persistence in these apostles?

Despite being beaten and charged "not to speak in the name of Jesus," the apostles "did not cease teaching and preaching that the Christ is Jesus." The mission Jesus has given them to be his witnesses and the Holy Spirit's power in them enables them to persevere with joy. Rather than being angry or disillusioned or dissuaded, they are outrageously happy to have suffered dishonor for the name of the Savior they love.

Perhaps they called to mind the things they had heard Jesus teach before his death, such as his promise that whoever loses his life for the sake of the gospel will save it (Mark 8:35). It must have been a great comfort to remember how Jesus had told them beforehand that they would suffer for bearing witness about him and to realize that he had kept his promise to send them a Helper (John 15:18–16:4).

9. Being beaten for speaking of Christ is likely outside of your experience, but suffering dishonor for speaking about or identifying with Jesus may not be. How difficult is it for you to imagine rejoicing in that? What fueled the apostles' rejoicing that could also enable you to rejoice?

Personal response.

Discussion Questions

1. In Acts 4:32 we read that this new community was "of one heart and soul." What would it be like to be part of a commu-

nity like this? What hinders this kind of unity in the church, both then and now?

Philippians 2 teaches us that selfish ambition, conceit, and self-centeredness are tremendous threats to unity. Where individuals are "looking out for number one," they cannot be "of one heart and soul" with others. Our unity is also threatened when we fail to keep the gospel of Jesus the main thing. If we instead elevate secondary issues, we will find ourselves focused on our disagreements rather than united in heart and soul. On a very practical level, unity is damaged by poor communication: failing to assume the best of others, not listening well, avoiding difficult conversations, or refusing to work through conflict in pursuit of peace.

2. How have you witnessed generosity among brothers and sisters in Christ? What are some ways you'd like to see more generosity in the church?

   Personal response.

3. When you read the story of Ananias and Sapphira, how do you find yourself responding emotionally? Are you horrified, offended, relieved, satisfied? Why?

   Personal response.

4. What are some things we might do or say to appear more spiritual than we really are? What motivates this kind of pretending?

   We might try to appear more spiritual than we really are by saying things like, "The Lord told me . . . ," implying that we have such a close relationship to God that he speaks to us extrabiblically. We could drop in that we are praying about something, when really we've just been thinking about it but haven't actually taken it to God in prayer. We might make sure that something we've done for someone, or some generosity on our part, is public by posting a picture of it or talking about it instead of doing our giving in secret (Matt. 6:3–4).

This pretending may be motivated by a fear of man rather than fear of the Lord—it could indicate that the opinions and approval of others are more important to you than honoring Jesus Christ.

5. Nancy said, "Jealousy is a terrible thing. Even worse is jealousy over the power and impact of someone else's genuine ministry impact." Have you ever felt this kind of jealousy, or had it directed toward you? What can we do to fight envy when we see God using someone else in a way we wish he was using us?

   The best thing we can do with jealousy, like any sin, is to run to Jesus with it. It's difficult to stew in envy and pray for the person you envy at the same time. Confess to the Lord how you're feeling and ask him to bless the ministry of the people you envy. Ask him to protect them from pride or other moral failure, to keep them humbly dependent on him, to multiply their fruit and continue using them to advance his kingdom. Then ask him to open your eyes to the ministry opportunities he has put in front of you today, however seemingly small. Ask for help to be faithful in whatever good work he has entrusted to you here and now.

6. The story of the new-covenant community has hardly gotten started when we read about this event with Ananias and Sapphira. And it is so much different than what we've read so far. What do you think Luke wants his readers to take away from it?

Luke concludes this story by saying that "great fear came upon the whole church and upon all who heard of these things" (Acts 5:11). In recounting these events, he hopes readers will know the same fear—the healthy fear of the Lord that comes from knowing who he is, what he expects of those who call themselves by his name, and what he is able to do. Like the early church, we too must sense the gravity of what it means to trifle with a holy God. We should hate any hint of this kind of hypocrisy in ourselves and ask the Spirit to work in us, making us people of integrity who fear him alone.

7. The religious council in Jerusalem seeks to silence the apostles through intimidation, imprisonment, and beatings. While many believers around the world face that exact treatment today, others face more subtle tactics. What are some other ways people seek to intimidate Christians and prevent them from speaking about Christ today?

In modern Western cultures, we typically don't face physical abuse or imprisonment for our faith. However, nonbelievers may seek to silence our proclamation of Christ by labeling it as intolerant, hateful, or backward. Professionals in certain careers may find their advancement hindered or have a hard time finding jobs.

8. How do you explain the apostles' response to being beaten in Acts 5:41–42?

Jesus is so real and so precious to the apostles and his suffering is so vivid in their memories that to suffer for the sake of his name feels like a gift. They remember his promise that whoever loses his life for the sake of the gospel will save it (Mark 8:35). Most of all, they rely on the power of the Spirit living within them. The Spirit fills them with love for God and love for people, as well as boldness, so that they are compelled to continue sharing the good news. They trust that this dishonor and physical beating is only temporary and will result in immeasurable eternal gain, both for them and for those who hear the gospel through their preaching.

9. While we may believe in theory that the gospel is unstoppable, sometimes it can be hard to believe this when we face opposition, or when we consider the opposition to the gospel around the world. What difference do you think it could make in your life, or in ministries that you are a part of, to really believe that the gospel is unstoppable?

Personal response.

Let's close by asking the Lord to show us any spiritual hypocrisy or ministry envy that needs to be confessed and forsaken. Let's ask him to fill us with courage to speak of him and supernatural joy when we suffer for doing so.

The Most High Does Not Dwell in Houses Made by Hands

ACTS 6:1–7:60

Personal Bible Study

1. Read Acts 6:1–7. According to verse 1 and verse 7, what is increasing?

   The number of disciples of Jesus and the word of God.

   What is the threat to the increase in these verses?

   Disunity because a certain people group is being overlooked.

2. Read Acts 6:7–12. What do you find in the following verses that might have generated anger toward Stephen and the gospel he was preaching among the Jews in Jerusalem?

   v. 7: *Many priests are forsaking their allegiance to the temple system and leaders to become part of this new community.*

v. 8: Stephen is doing signs and wonders among the people, demonstrating a compassion and power that the temple leaders don't have.

v. 10: They feel powerless in the face of Stephen's wisdom and the Spirit with which he speaks.

3. Read Acts 6:13–15. How would you summarize the charges against Stephen? How is what happens in verse 15 ironic in light of those charges? (See Ex. 34:29–35.)

   Stephen is charged with being against the temple and the law, even threatening to destroy the temple and change their way of life that they say came from Moses. It is ironic that while they accuse him of being against the law delivered by Moses, and wanting to change the customs delivered by Moses, Stephen suddenly looks like Moses did when he emerged from the presence of God on Mount Sinai (Ex. 34:34–35).

4. Read Acts 7:1–8. According to verse 2, where was the glory of God with Abraham?

   Mesopotamia.

5. Read Acts 7:9–16. According to verse 9, where was the presence of God with Joseph?

   Egypt.

6. Read Acts 7:17–36. According to verse 30, where was the glory of God with Moses?

   In a burning bush at Mount Sinai.

7. Read Acts 7:37–43. Why do you think Stephen mentions in verse 39 that Moses was rejected by the people?

He is showing that God's people have always rejected God's prophets. In rejecting Jesus, they have rejected the prophet Moses told them God would raise up. And now they are rejecting Stephen.

Why might Stephen specifically mention Aaron, the first high priest, leading the people into idolatry (v. 40)?

Stephen is speaking to the high priest, Annas, who (along with the other temple leaders) has led the people into idolatry. They have turned the temple itself into an idol, even as they have gone through the motions of worshiping God.

8. Read Acts 7:44–47. Where was the glory of God in Moses's day, in Joshua's day, in David's day, and in Solomon's day?

Moses' day (v. 44): *The tent of witness (or tabernacle) wandering in the wilderness.*

Joshua's day (v. 45): *The tabernacle went with the people throughout the promised land as they took possession of it.*

David's day (v. 45): *In the tabernacle.*

Solomon's day (v. 47): *In the temple in Jerusalem.*

9. Read Acts 7:48–50. According to Stephen, who quotes from Psalm 11 and Isaiah 66, where does God not dwell?

God does not dwell in houses made by hands. In other words, God cannot be confined to a building built by humans.

10. Read Acts 7:51–53. How would you summarize Stephen's final indictment of the religious leaders?

    You have stubbornly refused God. You may be circumcised in your body, but your inner life and lack of love for God show that you don't really belong to him. You are just like your ancestors who killed the prophets. You killed the one the prophets wrote about. You are accusing me of rejecting the law, but you have never kept it.

11. Read Acts 7:54–60. How is Stephen's declaration of what he sees a fitting conclusion to the argument he's been making?

    Stephen has been building an argument that the glory and presence of God has never been confined to the temple in Jerusalem. Now he gazes into heaven and sees the glory of God there, where Jesus is.

12. Following Stephen's interaction with his accusers and tracing his argument in this passage is rather challenging. Hopefully it will become clearer as you read Nancy's chapter or watch the video session. It ends, however, with the sad and yet victorious event of the stoning of Stephen. What aspects of the way Stephen faces death would you hope to emulate when facing death?

    Personal response.

Discussion Questions

1. How does Acts 6:7 provide a sort of "progress report" on the outworking of Acts 1:8? How do you think the temple leaders feel about these developments?

Acts 6:7 shows that by the power of the Holy Spirit, the apostolic witness is accomplishing its commission in Jerusalem. A significant number of people in the city are being saved. The fact that many of the priests are being saved shows the spread of the gospel—which would have been particularly enraging to the temple leaders. As large numbers of people and priests transfer their allegiance from the temple system to the new community of Jesus followers, the leaders likely feel their significance and power slipping away.

2. In many ways, the interaction between Stephen and his accusers is hard to follow. Just to make sure we're all clear, what are the two charges made against Stephen? And how would you summarize his response to those charges?

   Stephen is charged with speaking against the temple and the law of Moses—the place of God's presence and the source of God's word. His response is that God's presence, or glory, has never been confined to the temple in Jerusalem, that the people have never actually obeyed the law of Moses, and that the people have always killed God's prophets.

3. Think back through Stephen's argument (without looking, if you can!) and trace the location of God's presence or glory throughout Israel's history.

   - *Appeared to Abraham in Mesopotamia (city of Ur south of Babylon).*
   - *With Joseph in Egypt.*
   - *In the burning bush Moses saw in the wilderness of Mount Sinai.*
   - *On Mount Sinai as God came down to deliver his law to Moses.*

- *Tent of witness, or tabernacle, throughout the wilderness wandering and into the promised land.*
- *Temple built by Solomon in Jerusalem.*
- *Heaven's throne room (according to the quote of Isa. 66:1–2 in Acts 7:49).*

4. What do we learn about God as we trace where his presence moved throughout the history of his people? (For a clear statement of God's intention, see Ex. 29:45–46.)

God is committed to his people and wants to be with his people. This is amazing! The one true God who made the world desires—in fact is determined—to dwell among his people.

5. Where is God's presence or glory found today? How does this reality challenge or encourage you?

God's glory dwells in heaven, but he also dwells in and with his people. This should cause us to want to live lives of holiness that are pleasing to him. It should encourage us to know that the God of the universe really does condescend to dwell with and within us. He loves us enough to want to be with us. His presence with us provides comfort, guidance, and courage. We can face death knowing that when we die and our spirits go to be with Christ, we will experience his presence and glory in an even more immediate and tangible way.

6. Why is it likely not surprising to Stephen that they want to kill him?

Stephen is well aware of the long history of God's people mistreating his prophets, as well as the more recent history of Jesus's suffering and death. He has also seen the imprisonment and beating of the apostles. As a follower of Jesus and one who speaks his words, Stephen knows he might be treated in the same way.

7. What might have comforted Stephen as he faced death?

As he faced death, the example of Jesus and the promises of glory after suffering gave Stephen strength to suffer and be killed with great faith and grace toward his persecutors. He was experiencing the very phenomenon Paul described in Philippians 3:10, the fellowship of sharing in Christ's suffering. Seeing the glory of Jesus, with Jesus standing in heaven as if to welcome him and represent him before the Father, would have been an incredible source of strength and hope.

8. How can Stephen's death provide comfort to us as believers in life and in death?

Knowing that we are filled with the same Spirit that filled Stephen, we are encouraged to believe that we can face death with the same courage, peace, and even care for others. Stephen's words help us believe that the glory on the other side of suffering is real and beautiful, worth whatever it may cost us in this life. We can also note that in the midst of such violence, Stephen's death is so peaceful that it is described as falling asleep. Perhaps this can take away some of our fear of death.

Let's close by praying for our brothers and sisters around the world who face the kind of treatment Stephen suffered—that they would have courage to stand firm in their faith and joy as they anticipate seeing his glory.

Lesson 6

They Were All Scattered

ACTS 8:1–40

Personal Bible Study

1. Read Acts 7:59–8:4. How is the persecution that comes upon the church after the death of Stephen a demonstration or illustration of Joseph's words to his brothers in Genesis 50:20: "As for you, you meant evil against me, but God meant it for good, to bring it about that many people should be kept alive, as they are today"?

   Those who persecute the believers in Jerusalem following the death of Stephen clearly mean evil against them. The believers' suffering is profound and significant. Yet God means it for good, as a catalyst for the spread of the gospel beyond Jerusalem. We can always be sure that God is sovereignly at work in the suffering of his people to fulfill his salvation purposes.

2. Read Luke 9:51–56 and John 4:5–9. How does seeing the at-titude of the apostles toward Samaritans in these passages help us to understand the significance of what we read in Acts 8:5–8?

The apostles, like all Jews, hated Samaritans and wanted nothing to do with them. James and John seem perfectly happy for them to burn up in judgment. But God is at work in and through Philip, giving him a desire to bring the gospel to Samaritans and using him to welcome them into the wholeness and health of being in Christ. We might wonder if "much joy" had ever been the result of Jews visiting their city before. But things have changed because of the love that Philip is extending to them.

3. Read Acts 8:9–13. What are some key differences between Simon and Philip? Pay special attention to the words or con-cepts that show up in both the description of Simon (vv. 9–11) and the description of Philip (vv. 12–13).

Simon speaks of his own greatness and great name; Philip speaks of the good news about the kingdom of God and the name of Jesus Christ. The people think Simon's power is from God, when really it is from Satan. Philip's signs and miracles are empowered by God.

4. Read Acts 8:14–17. Why would it have been important for the apostles to witness the Samaritans receiving the Holy Spirit in a way similar to the experience of believers in Jerusalem on Pentecost?

Given the longstanding animosity between Jews and Samaritans, the Jewish apostles (the chief eyewitnesses charged with proclaiming the gospel message) need eyewitness confirmation that the Spirit has been poured out on Samaritans as well as Jews. They need to see that the same Holy Spirit is at work in the Samaritans, making them part of the same covenant community with the Jewish believers.

5. Read Acts 8:18–24. Commentators disagree regarding whether or not Simon came to genuine faith in Christ. What evidence do you see for and against it here?

In verse 13, we're told that Simon believed and was baptized, that he continued listening to and observing Philip, and that he was amazed by what he heard and saw. When he is confronted about his sin, Simon asks Peter to pray for him. But the fact that he wants to pay the apostles money so that he can add another trick to his trade seems to indicate that he did not truly experience a miracle of grace and mercy. Peter's words, "May your silver perish with you," seem to indicate that Simon is going to perish rather than live. Peter says Simon's heart is not right before God and calls upon him to repent. He also uses Old Testament language, saying that Simon has "neither part nor lot in this matter," which seems to suggest that Simon has no place of belonging in the new-covenant community but is instead "in the bond of iniquity" (still bound up in sin).

6. Read Acts 8:25. What aspect of Jesus's command in Acts 1:8 are Peter and John fulfilling?

Jesus had called the apostles to be his witnesses to the Jew first and then to Judea and Samaria. They are taking the gospel deep into Samaria.

7. Read Acts 8:26–28. What do you think this Gentile eunuch likely experienced when he went to the temple in Jerusalem? (See Deut. 23:1 for help.)

   Though he had come to Jerusalem to worship the one true God, he was likely barred from entering the temple because he was a Gentile and a eunuch. But it doesn't seem to have discouraged him, as he is reading the scroll of the prophet Isaiah and seeking to understand it.

8. How might the Ethiopian eunuch have found hope in the following Old Testament passages? (Note that Cush is the ancient name for the territory of the Ethiopians.)

   Psalm 68:31: "Cush shall hasten to stretch out her hands to God."

   Psalm 87:4: "Among those who know me I mention . . . Cush."

   Isaiah 56:3–5: Eunuchs who hold fast to God's covenant will be accepted into God's eternal house. They will be given something even better than sons and daughters—a name that will not be cut off—which means that they will never be rejected.

9. Read Acts 8:29–38 along with Isaiah 53. Philip tells the eunuch the good news about Jesus based on the passage he is reading in Isaiah 53. What might Philip have said about Jesus based on Isaiah 53?

   He might have said, "This passage is about the suffering servant, Jesus of Nazareth, who was crucified just a short time ago in Jerusalem. He was despised and rejected, like you were in Jerusalem. The world saw his death as a great humiliation, but in reality it was his great exaltation. The world saw only agony and defeat, but it was actually a glorious victory. The servant's suffering was purposeful. Indeed God was at work in his death to accomplish his good purposes for people like me and you. 'Yet it was the will of the LORD to crush him; he has put him to grief' (Isa. 53:10). God says that through the death of 'the righteous one, my servant,' many will be 'accounted righteous, and he shall bear their iniquities' (Isa. 53:11). You too can be 'accounted righteous,' by becoming united to Jesus Christ, the righteous one, by faith."

10. In this chapter, Philip takes the gospel to people he would have avoided all his life. Are there any types or categories of people you would find it especially hard to share Christ with? What do you think it would take for you to move toward such people in love?

    Personal response.

Discussion Questions

1. Read Ezekiel 37:15–19 together. How is this becoming reality in Acts 8?

   The people of Samaria are descendants of the ten northern tribes taken into exile by Assyria and intermarried with people of other nations. In other words, they are the "stick of Joseph." The Jews would be the "stick of Judah," the descendants of the southern kingdom who came back from exile in Babylon. These two "sticks," or people groups, have been alienated from each other for centuries. But in Acts 8, Philip takes the gospel to Samaria. And as Peter and John come to lay hands on the Samaritans to receive the Holy Spirit, the two "sticks," or those from the two people groups who have put their faith in Jesus, are being made into one stick, one people of God.

2. Imagine that you are a Samaritan living in Samaria when Philip comes to town. What kinds of things are you hearing and witnessing? By the time Philip, Peter, and John leave, how has your life changed?

   To begin with, you might not be able to get over the fact that a faithful Jew has made his way to the city just to interact with you! That's never happened before.

   Since Samaritans have only the books of Moses, perhaps Philip focuses on presenting Jesus as the Christ from those specific books. Perhaps you hear him preach Jesus as the second Adam, the promised Son, the one who rescues his people from slavery to sin, the once for all sacrifice, the God who tabernacled among us, the holy one of God who makes us holy, the one who perfectly obeyed in our place.

   You would be seeing people who have suffered their whole lifetime with sickness, paralysis, and lameness being healed. People who have lost their minds, whose lives have been destroyed from being inhabited by demons, are being cleansed and set free to live a normal life.

   Two leaders from the church in Jerusalem come to lay hands on you, and you experience the indwelling of the Holy Spirit, sealing you to Christ and empowering you to live a whole new life in relationship with Jesus.

You have a new sense of identity. You're no longer a Samaritan completely alienated from Jews. You have brothers and sisters in Jerusalem. You are joined with them in this new community of those who belong to Jesus.

3. In what ways is Jesus a gatherer? Consider his earthly ministry, death, resurrection, ascension, sending his Spirit, present reign, and promised return.

   In fulfillment of the Old Testament prophets, Jesus is a gatherer in terms of being a king over one kingdom and reuniting the twelve tribes of Israel in the new community of believers. During his earthly ministry, Jesus gathered a diverse group of twelve disciples and other followers to himself. He interacted with the lowly as well as the rich and powerful. He ate with tax collectors and sinners. In his dying words, he assured one of the thieves being crucified beside him that this thief would be with him in paradise. His death, resurrection, and ascension have a gathering effect on all who put their hope in him. By his Spirit and through his word, Jesus continues to gather a people for himself from every tribe, tongue, and nation. One day when he returns, he will gather his own to live with him forever in the new creation.

4. Nancy confessed that she has a long way to go to be a gatherer like Jesus is a gatherer. Can you relate to that? What steps could you take to become more of a gatherer like Jesus?

   Personal response.

5. In what ways is Simon the magician similar to Achan (Josh. 7:10–21), Judas (Matt. 26:14–16), and Ananias and Sapphira (Acts 5:1–11)? What does this indicate about him?

Achan was part of the people of God taking possession of the promised land. Rather than obey the Lord's command to devote to destruction everything in the city of Jericho, he hid some of the treasures in his tent and was put to death because of it.

Judas was among the twelve disciples, but he clearly loved money more than he loved Jesus, betraying him for money and perishing alienated from Christ.

Ananias and Sapphira demonstrated their love of money by misrepresenting their gift to the needs of other believers, keeping back some for themselves. They died instantly.

Simon is similar to these in appearing to be devoted to the purposes of God while demonstrating a desire to enrich himself. This indicates that he is likely a false believer who seeks to use God for selfish gain rather than to serve God as his ultimate treasure.

We can't be adamant about the falseness of Simon and his eternal destiny, however, since the text is somewhat ambiguous. But Peter's words, "May your silver perish with you," and, "You have neither part nor lot" in the matters of the Spirit, as well as his plea with Simon to repent, seem to indicate that although we read earlier that Simon believed (v. 13), perhaps it was not saving faith.

6. Nancy challenged us to examine ourselves rather than focus on Simon the magician. What are some ways people might be tempted to use Jesus for their own ends rather than loving and serving Jesus because he is worthy of devotion?

Some people can be drawn into ministry with greater interest in making money than in serving Christ or serving people (though most people in ministry sacrifice income to serve). But every believer can face the temptation to present herself as more spiritual, more generous, or more sacrificial in her giving or service than she really is to gain the admiration of others.

Perhaps we are tempted to buy into the lies of the prosperity gospel, following Jesus in hopes that he will give us health, wealth, and earthly happiness. We want to serve Jesus, but what we really want is a satisfying marriage, or an admirable family, or vocational success. Rather than love and worship Jesus for who he is, we look for what we can get out of it—focused more on the gifts than on the giver. Sometimes our prayers are more oriented toward what will bring us comfort or pleasure, what will make our lives easier, rather than toward what will bring him glory.

7. In the personal Bible study, you were asked to take a stab at writing out how Philip might have explained the good news of Jesus to the Ethiopian eunuch from Isaiah 53. Would any of you be willing to share what you wrote or take a stab at it if you didn't write something?

Here is a sample: "This passage is about the suffering servant, Jesus of Nazareth, who was crucified just a short time ago in

Jerusalem. He was despised and rejected, like you were in Jerusalem. The world saw his death as a great humiliation, but in reality it was his great exaltation. The world saw only agony and defeat, but it was actually a glorious victory. The servant's suffering was purposeful. Indeed God was at work in his death to accomplish his good purposes for people like me and you. 'Yet it was the will of the LORD to crush him; he has put him to grief' (Isa. 53:10). God says that through the death of 'the righteous one, my servant,' many will be 'accounted righteous, and he shall bear their iniquities' (Isa. 53:11). You too can be 'accounted righteous,' by becoming united to Jesus Christ, the righteous one, by faith."

8. In Acts 8, we see Philip share the gospel of Jesus with despised outsiders and unwanted outcasts in his day. Of course, there are despised outsiders and unwanted outcasts in our day as well. What do you think it takes for us to overcome our prejudice, arrogance, or apathy so that we are willing to share the gospel with these outsiders and outcasts? What do we have that Philip had?

We need to see that we were unworthy outsiders and outcasts. Nothing in us made us worthy of the love of Christ: "While we were enemies we were reconciled to God by the death of his Son" (Rom. 5:10). When we consider how grace and love have been extended to us, that grace and love we've received can overflow to those we might not be drawn to. The same Holy Spirit who filled Philip is at work in us, enabling us to die to ourselves and our preferences and to love the way Christ loves.

It can be difficult for us to admit, even to ourselves, that there are categories of people we avoid, dislike, or even despise. Let's pray that we would have the eyes to recognize our blind spots in regard to our own prejudices and ask the Lord for humility and grace to grow in love for all people.

Lesson 7

God's Chosen Instrument

ACTS 9:1–31

Personal Bible Study

1. What do we learn about Saul's background from the following passages?

Philippians 3:4–6: *He is a "Hebrew of Hebrews," with every reason for confidence in the flesh: circumcised; able to trace his lineage from the tribe of Benjamin; a blameless, law-keeping Pharisee; a zealous persecutor of the church.*

Acts 7:57–8:3: *He presided over the execution of Stephen and ravaged the church, breaking into homes and dragging men and women off to prison.*

Acts 22:3–5: *He is a Jew, born in Tarsus, raised in Jerusalem, and educated strictly under Gamaliel. He was so zealous for God that he persecuted Christians to the death, binding and delivering men and women, traveling long distances to chase and punish them. (The ESV Study Bible notes: "'Brought up in this city' most likely means that Paul's parents moved to Jerusalem when he was very young and he was reared in the city . . . but some take it to mean only that Paul came to Jerusalem as a young man for his rabbinic training under Gamaliel.")*[1]

2. How do Leviticus 24:16 and John 16:2–3 help us to understand what motivates Saul in his rage against those who put their faith in Jesus?

Saul thinks he is being obedient and faithful to God in putting blasphemers to death as the law prescribes. Saul thinks that by killing followers of Jesus, he is "offering service to God."

3. Read Acts 9:1–2. What words would you use to describe Saul's attitude and actions?

Saul seems to ooze murderous hostility toward those who follow Jesus. He's aggressive in wanting to find them, bind them in chains, and bring them (perhaps drag them) back to Jerusalem, where they will stand before the Sanhedrin and likely be condemned to death. He seems to relish being a part of their deaths.

4. Read Acts 9:3–9. Why would it be devastating for Saul to hear that the person speaking to him out of the radiant, blinding light from heaven is Jesus of Nazareth?

---

1   *ESV Study Bible*, ed. Wayne Grudem (Wheaton, IL: Crossway, 2008), note on Acts 22:3.

Saul has devoted his life to a cause he believes is righteous, only to find out that it is actually the opposite of righteous. Rather than honoring God by persecuting and killing blasphemers, he himself is the blasphemer acting in opposition to God. His zeal is entirely misdirected; all along, he has been fighting against the Lord. For Saul to hear directly from the risen and ascended Jesus means that he has gotten it all wrong, that Jesus is exactly who he said he was. And Jesus takes the persecution of those joined to him personally—which means Saul is accountable for tremendous wrongdoing.

5. According to 1 Corinthians 9:1 and Acts 9:27, what or who creates the blinding light that temporarily blinds Saul?

Saul is blinded by seeing the light of the glory of the risen and ascended Jesus.

6. Read Acts 9:10–22. While something supernatural is happening to Saul on the road to Damascus, something supernatural is also happening to Ananias in Damascus. What happens, and why do you think it is necessary?

The Lord speaks to Ananias in a vision, telling him what has happened to Saul and instructing him to go to Saul and restore his sight. Ananias would need such a supernatural revelation to seek out someone who was actively trying to kill him and his fellow believers. He must have truly believed what was revealed to him, since he addresses Saul as "brother." The scales falling from Saul's eyes must have been a visible sign of his spiritual blindness falling away, so that he is received and baptized as a fellow believer in Christ.

7. What do you think Ananias and the other disciples of Jesus in Damascus must have thought and felt when they heard Saul declaring in the synagogue that Jesus was the Son of God?

Given that Ananias heard directly from God about this, he was probably filled with joy and amazement. For the other disciples, there was likely some fear and cynicism and skepticism mixed in. But it was also a demonstration of the awesome power and sovereignty of God, and as such, it would be an encouragement that God can use anyone to fulfill his plan. Perhaps it was also a helpful reminder of the continuity between the God of the old covenant and the church under Jesus Christ—to see him working now the same way he had worked throughout human history, choosing the least likely people to accomplish his purposes in the world.

8. What is emphasized in both Acts 9:15 and Galatians 1:11–16 about Paul's ministry?

Paul was chosen by God to take the gospel to the Gentiles. God tells Ananias that Saul is his "chosen instrument" to carry his name to the Gentiles. In Galatians, Paul writes that Jesus revealed himself directly to him because he had chosen Paul before he was even born to preach Christ among the Gentiles.

9. Read Acts 9:23–31. What is ironic in this passage in terms of what is happening to the man who sought to kill followers of Jesus?

The hunter has become the hunted. The one who was seeking to kill those belonging to the Way is now being sought so that he might be put to death.

10. To the Christians in his day, Saul must have seemed like the last person in the world who would ever become a Christian. Are there any people like that in your world? Spend some time praying that the same Jesus who revealed himself to Saul would reveal himself to those who are blind to who he is.

Discussion Questions

Note: This lesson has fewer discussion questions than most to allow extra time for sharing on the final question.

1. What stood out to you as you read this story of Saul's experience on the road to Damascus, whether you were hearing it for the first time or rereading a well-known passage?

Personal response.

2. Imagine yourself as Ananias. What might you have thought or felt when the Lord told you to go lay hands on Saul? What would it have been like for the other believers in Damascus to hear about Saul's conversion? (Consider that some of them may have known Stephen or had loved ones who were persecuted and killed in Jerusalem.)

Word of Saul's murderous threats had spread all the way to Damascus so that Ananias and his fellow believers were likely full of fear. We can imagine them praying that Saul would not lay hands on them to drag them away. For Ananias to be told to go seek out this persecutor and lay hands on him—not to harm him, but to heal him—must have been shocking! Perhaps since he received a vision directly from God, Ananias could have been filled with joy and amazement. Yet he was human, so we could understand if he felt fear, cynicism, or skepticism mixed in. Could it really be true that Saul would become a follower of Jesus?

Other believers likely would have experienced the same range of emotions. For many, it could have been incredibly painful and difficult to hear that the man who had murdered your loved one was now the object of God's special favor. On the other hand, those with great faith might have been able to rejoice at this demonstration of God's sovereign power. What an incredible reminder that God can use anyone to fulfill his plans! Just as he had under the old covenant, God was choosing the least likely person to accomplish his purposes in the world.

3. If you were a believer in Saul's day, how do you think you might have felt about welcoming him into your church? What do you think it was like for Saul to have relationships with believers he had persecuted? What would both sides have needed for those relationships to flourish?

    It is often said that forgiveness is not a one-time act but a decision that must be made again and again—an act that is empowered and motivated by the grace and forgiveness we've received from Jesus. If Paul (Saul) had killed your friends or family members, you would need grace to keep making the choice to forgive him. To do so, you would have to keep looking to the cross and reminding yourself of the fact that your own sins crucified Jesus just as much as Paul's did. You would have to believe that the same forgiveness you received from Christ had been extended to Paul. You would have to trust the Holy Spirit at work in Paul and believe in the sovereign goodness of God in spite of your loss. Reminding yourself of the glory that your loved ones were enjoying in the presence of Christ would probably help.

Paul would have needed a tremendous amount of ongoing humility to face these brothers and sisters he had hurt so deeply. He would have needed to confess his sin to them and ask their forgiveness, to love and serve them. At the same time, he too would need to keep looking to the cross, not as a reminder of his sin but as a reminder of God's grace. He would have to trust that Jesus's work of redemption covered all his sins and that there was no condemnation for him any longer, that he did not have to bear shame over his past because Jesus had borne it for him.

4. Read Galatians 1:11–16 together. What are some implications of the fact that God chose Paul to preach Christ among the Gentiles before he was even born? What does this tell us about God's sovereignty over salvation and his providence in our lives?

It demonstrates that God is supremely sovereign over his world and that he is able and determined to work out his plans for salvation in his way and in his timing. If God chose Paul before he was born and was sovereign over his salvation, we have to reckon with the reality that God was sovereign over Paul's years of unbelief, blasphemy, and cruel, murderous persecution of believers. We may never be able to fully understand God's delays in saving, his willingness to allow his people to endure suffering and even death for their allegiance to him. But we must trust that he is working out his plans for salvation in this world and in our lives, and that his plans will be for our good and for his glory.

5. Nancy said that when a person is saved, it is always supernatural, though it might appear to be quite ordinary. It doesn't have to be sensational or emotional to be supernatural. Some people can tell you the moment when everything changed, and they became clear on who Jesus is. Others can't tell you exactly when it happened. But that doesn't mean it didn't. How does this encourage you or challenge you in your understanding of conversion?

Personal response.

6. Are there any members of this group who would be willing to share about your own conversion? How did you go from being spiritually dead to spiritually alive?

Personal response.

Before we pray, would anyone like to share the names of particular people you want us to ask God to supernaturally save? Let's pray together for the salvation of those people.

What God Has Made Clean

ACTS 9:32–11:18

Personal Bible Study

1. Read Acts 9:32–35 and Luke 5:18–26. What similarities do you see between the healing Jesus performed in Luke's Gospel and the healing Jesus performed through Peter?

   They are both told to rise and deal with their beds.

   They both arise.

   Those who witness the miracle are amazed/turn to/glorify God.

2. Read Acts 9:36–42 and Mark 5:35–43. What similarities do you see between the healing Jesus performed in Mark's Gospel and the healing Jesus performed through Peter? What is the big difference at the end?

They were both urged to go to the home where someone was dying/dead.

They both went even though the person had died.

When they arrived, people were weeping.

They told most or all other people to leave the room.

They both took the dead person by the hand and said, "Talitha/ Tabitha, arise."

They both immediately got up.

The difference: while Jesus told people not to tell others about his miracle, Peter's miracle became known, and many believed in the Lord.

3. Why do you think Luke might have told the stories about the miracles Peter performed in such a similar way to the stories of Jesus's earlier miracles?

   He wants us to see that Peter's ministry is a continuation of Jesus's ministry. Peter therefore has the same power and purpose as well as apostolic authority.

4. Read Acts 10:1–8. Cornelius is a Gentile, but he is not like most Gentiles. What sets him apart from most Gentiles and makes him similar to the Ethiopian eunuch we met in chapter 8?

   Cornelius is a devout God fearer who gives generously and prays continually. He worships the God of Israel, but he does not yet understand the gospel of Christ.

5. To understand why Peter's vision and experience in Acts 10 is so significant, we have to go back to the Mosaic law. Skim Leviticus 11:1–19, 45–47. Then read Exodus 19:4–6; Deuteronomy 4:5–8; and Jeremiah 33:8–9. What do these passages reveal about God's purpose in setting apart the Israelites to be his "treasured possession" from among the nations and giving them the holiness laws in Leviticus?

When the Mosaic law was given, the Israelites were on their way to take possession of the land of Canaan from the pagan Canaanites. They were to "be holy" as God is holy. This means that they were to be distinct in their behavior, to separate themselves from the pagan rituals and practices of the surrounding nations. In doing so, they would reflect God's holiness—his "set-apart-ness," the way he is entirely different from and far above the pagan gods. One way they could demonstrate that separation was in what they ate. Their diet would be noticeably different from the pagan nations around them, which would serve as a reminder at every meal that they were God's holy people.

As his "treasured possession" among all peoples, the Israelites were to serve as "a kingdom of priests"—in other words, they would be mediators, bringing the goodness and glory of God to all other people groups. They were to be set apart to God in such a way that people of other nations would be attracted to Israel's God. As other nations saw God's goodness to his people, other nations would fear and tremble before Israel's God.

6. What practical effect would the food laws have had on Jewish interaction with Gentiles?

The food laws made social mixing with Gentiles difficult, since Israelites could not eat Gentile food. This would not only reinforce the fact that Israel was a special nation, but also act as a constant reminder that Israel was to avoid the moral and spiritual uncleanness of the Gentiles.

7. Read Acts 10:9–16. In light of what you read in Leviticus 11, why do you think the divine voice repeats his instruction to Peter three times?

   It seems significant that "you shall not eat" is repeated three times in Leviticus 11 (vv. 4, 8, 11). This would have been a huge change from something that had been at the center of Peter's life and the lives of his people for centuries. Eating only clean animals was a point of pride for Jewish people. Because of the clear, repeated Old Testament command to not eat of the forbidden animals, Peter would have needed to be very sure that the new message was from God if he was going to obey it.

8. Read Acts 10:17–23. What do you think would have happened differently if Peter had not just received the vision from God?

   Peter likely would not have invited Gentile servants in as guests, nor would he have gone with them to a Gentile's home.

9. Read Acts 10:24–33. What does Peter's statement in verse 28 reveal about how he has interpreted the vision given to him in Joppa?

   Peter understands that if God has declared all foods clean, then all people are likewise clean. He understands that he should no longer refuse to associate with Gentiles.

10. Read Peter's gospel announcement to the Gentiles gathered in Cornelius's home in Acts 10:34–43. What are the key elements of his gospel presentation?

- *The gospel is for all nations.*
- *Jesus's healing ministry.*
- *Jesus's death as cursed by God.*
- *His resurrection and post-resurrection appearances.*
- *His present reign as judge of the living and the dead.*
- *Everyone who believes in Jesus receives forgiveness of sins.*

11. Read Acts 10:44–48. If the Gentiles who believe the gospel receive the same gift as the Jews who believed the gospel back in Acts 2, what does this mean for the future of the new-covenant community?

    It will include both Jews and Gentiles as full members of the people of God, with no division or favoritism.

12. Read Acts 11:1–18. How does the attitude of some of the Jews in Jerusalem change from verse 2 to verse 18?

    Initially, the "circumcision party" (those who insist that anyone who wants to become a Christian must become a Jew first) are critical of Peter's association with Gentiles in Caesarea. But after hearing Peter's story, they fall silent. Then they glorify God, recognizing that God has granted repentance and eternal life to the Gentiles.

13. Acts 11:18 celebrates that God has granted the Gentiles "repentance that leads to life." How would you define repentance?

In what ways does it lead to life? How have you personally experienced repentance leading to life?

Repentance is a turning away from sin and self toward Christ in faith and obedience. Throughout the book of Acts, repentance is a change of mind in regard to Jesus Christ—a turning away from unbelief and toward wholehearted belief in Jesus as the only source of salvation. This repentance leads to life in that it is a rejection of a life of sin or a life of seeking salvation through law-keeping or good deeds, which is life-depleting and defeating. Repentance, instead, is the embrace of the abundant and eternal life that is in Christ alone.

Discussion Questions

1. To really understand what transpired in this lesson, it helps to make sure we're clear on the Old Testament background for it. What was God's purpose in setting apart the Israelites to be his "treasured possession" from among the nations and giving them the holiness laws in Leviticus? How did the Jews misuse or misunderstand this?

   When the Mosaic law was given, the Israelites were on their way to take possession of the land of Canaan from the pagan Canaanites. They were to "be holy" as God is holy. This meant that they were to be distinct in their behavior, to separate themselves from the pagan rituals and practices of the surrounding nations. In doing so, they would reflect God's holiness—his "set-apart-ness," the way he is entirely different from and far above the pagan gods. One way they could demonstrate that separation was in what they ate. Their diet would be noticeably different from the pagan nations around them, which would serve as a reminder at every meal that they were God's holy people.

These food laws had an immediate practical effect: they made social mixing with Gentiles difficult, since Israelites could not eat Gentile food. But rather than seeing their status of being set apart as a means to the goal of drawing all people to God, the Jews saw holiness as an end in and of itself. Privilege led to pride—the kind of pride that caused Jewish people to look down on and even despise Gentiles. The food laws that made it difficult to share a meal with Gentiles became an excuse to detest and avoid Gentiles. Instead of embracing their role as God's instrument to draw all peoples, they embraced prejudice against all peoples.

2. Though we do not live under the Mosaic law, we have the same calling to be holy. What does it mean for Christians to pursue holiness? How can we avoid the errors of the first-century Jews?

   To be holy means that we are "set apart for honorable use." Paul wrote to Timothy, "Therefore, if anyone cleanses himself from what is dishonorable, he will be a vessel for honorable use, set apart as holy, useful to the master of the house, ready for every good work" (2 Tim. 2:21). When we are joined to Christ, we are immediately made holy. At the same time, the entire Christian life is a process of growing in holiness. God has given us his Spirit so that we can overcome temptation and become more and more conformed to the image of Christ, manifesting the fruit of the Spirit. Ultimately, holiness for the Christian is not about following a list of rules but about pursuing the person of Jesus and maturing to look more like him.

To avoid the errors of the first-century Jews, we need to think less about outward appearances and more about genuine purity of thought, motive, and action. We also need to avoid self-righteousness that looks down on those we consider to be less holy than we are. Always we must keep in mind the goal of pursuing holiness: to honor the Lord by displaying his character to others, and hopefully to draw them to know and love Jesus Christ.

3. Why do you think it requires divine revelation—repeated three times—for Peter to change how he sees the consumption of unclean animals?

   This would have been a huge change from something that had been at the center of Peter's life and the life of his people for centuries. It was a point of pride for Jewish people in general, and for Peter in particular. It is a significant shift to be able to eat unclean food and commune as an equal with the Gentile Cornelius. Because the Old Testament command not to eat of the forbidden animals was emphasized and repeated, Peter would have needed to be very sure that the new message was from God if he was going to obey it.

4. Why is Peter's vision a necessary step in the fulfillment of Jesus's commission in Acts 1:8 ("You will be my witnesses in Jerusalem and in all Judea and Samaria, and to the end of the earth")?

   If the apostles were not willing to go into Gentile spaces with the offer of salvation, they would not have been able to fulfill their calling as witnesses to the end of the earth.

5. Peter concludes by asking, "Who was I that I could stand in God's way?" (Acts 11:17). How might we "stand in God's way" of welcoming people into Christ's church today?

Perhaps our tribalism hinders us from being welcoming to all. Insisting on total agreement in secondary issues before accepting other believers as genuine brothers and sisters in Christ could be a form of trying to "stand in God's way."

And perhaps we sometimes communicate to outsiders embracing the gospel for the first time that they must deal with all of their sin before they can be accepted into our fellowship. We could "stand in God's way" if we require that they clean themselves up first, rather than welcoming them on the basis of their desire to forsake sin and grow in holiness.

6. Acts 11:18 celebrates that God has granted the Gentiles "repentance that leads to life." How would you define *repentance*? In what ways does it lead to life?

Repentance is not a fleeting attempt to reform certain behaviors in our lives. It is a radical reorientation of our allegiance and devotion. The outpouring of the Spirit is a divine and inerrant indicator that God has given these Gentiles just such repentance.

The word repent *literally means "to turn"—a complete change of direction. Repentance leads to life because it is a turning away from sin, which brings only death (Rom. 6:23; James 1:15), and turning toward Christ, who is our life (John 14:6; Col. 3:4). We're revived as we forsake what only takes from us and works destruction in our lives. We're given hope and peace and joy as we pursue Christ and grow more like him.*

7. Would anyone in the group be willing to share a personal experience of repentance leading to life?

Personal response.

Let's pray, asking God to grant us ongoing repentance that leads to life.

Lesson 9

The Hand of the Lord
Was with Them

ACTS 11:19–12:25

Personal Bible Study

1. Read Acts 11:19–20. Note these locations on a map. Up to this point, the Jewish believers have been preaching Christ to Jews and God-fearing Gentiles (such as the Ethiopian eunuch and Cornelius). But as the gospel spreads out from Jerusalem geographically, it is also spreading out in terms of the people who are hearing it. What kind of people are now hearing the gospel, according to these verses?

Some of these Jewish believers are preaching about Christ to pagan Gentiles (Greek-speaking non-Jews). Note that while "Hellenists" in 6:1 and 9:29 referred to Greek-speaking Jews, Luke draws a contrast in 11:19–20 to indicate that the Hellenists here are not Jews. Nor are we given any reason to assume that they are God-fearing Gentiles. So we can assume they are pagan Gentiles.

2. Read Acts 11:19–26. Use the following chart to compare what happens as pagan Gentiles believe in Christ to what happened in Acts 8, when Samaritans believed in Christ.

	Acts 8 (Samaria)	Acts 11 (Antioch)
What precipitates the believers' departure from Jerusalem	A great persecution arises against the church after the stoning of Stephen. (8:1)	*Believers are scattered because of the persecution that arises over Stephen. (11:19)*
The kind of people to whom they present Christ	Philip preaches Christ to Samaritans (people who were partly Jewish). (8:4–6)	*Some preach Christ only to Jews living in Phoenicia, Cyprus, and Antioch. But some men of Cyprus and Cyrene speak to pagan Gentiles in Antioch. (11:19–20)*
The response to their message	Crowds listen and believe and are baptized. (8:12)	*A great number believe and turn to the Lord. (11:21)*
Apostolic authentication and support from Jerusalem elders	Peter and John are sent from Jerusalem to verify that Samaritans have become believers in Christ, to pray for them, and to lay hands on them to receive the Holy Spirit. (8:14–17)	*Barnabas is sent from Jerusalem to verify that pagan Gentiles have become believers in Christ. He exhorts them and then brings Saul to them. Barnabas and Saul spend a year teaching the new Christians. (11:22–26)*

3. Read Acts 11:27–30. What evidence do you see in these verses that the Spirit is at work in Antioch?

The Spirit enables Agabus to foresee a coming famine. The Spirit generates tremendous generosity in the hearts of the believers in Antioch, prompting them to send aid to brothers and sisters living in Judea that they had never met.

4. Read Acts 12:1–5. How is Herod Agrippa's treatment of James and Peter similar to the way Jesus was treated by Herod Antipas and Pilate in terms of motive, timing, and guarding?

Pilate agreed to kill Jesus to please the Jews. Herod Antipas wanted to kill Jesus. (Mark 15:15; Luke 13:31)	*Herod Agrippa killed James and sought to kill Peter to please the Jews.*
The arrest and killing of Jesus took place during the days of Unleavened Bread and Passover, motivated in part by Pilate's desire to appear to honor these Jewish feasts. (Mark 15:6; Luke 22:1–2)	*The killing of James and arrest of Peter took place during the days of Unleavened Bread and Passover, motivated in part by Agrippa's desire to appear to honor these Jewish feasts.*
Additional guards were added to secure Jesus's tomb, which could not hold him. (Matt. 27:65–66)	*Additional squads of soldiers were added to guard Peter, but the prison could not hold him.*

5. Read Acts 12:6–11. How do we see God accomplishing Peter's rescue?

Peter seems to need to be led and instructed by the angel of the Lord at every step while in a fog. He says he was rescued by the Lord, who "sent his angel."

6. Read Acts 12:12–19, then look back at verse 5. What do you find a bit ironic in this passage? Can you relate in any way to those gathered in prayer?

The believers are all praying for Peter's release, but when the answer to their prayers—a released Peter—knocks on the door, initially they don't believe it is him! Perhaps many of us can relate to earnestly praying for something while having little faith that our prayers will be or are being answered.

7. Read Acts 12:20–23. When Cornelius tried to worship Peter in Acts 10:25–26, Peter refused his worship and said, "I too

am a man," refusing to receive glory that belongs to God alone. How is Herod's response to being worshiped as a god in 12:20–23 different from that of Peter?

Herod did not reject being worshiped as a god and did not correct his worshipers to state that he was just a man. He "did not give God the glory" (12:23).

8. Read Acts 12:24. Why is this statement significant, considering the context of what we've read in chapter 12?

We might expect that the killing of James and the arrest of Peter would discourage the believers in Jerusalem from speaking the word of God and discourage unbelievers from wanting to become a part of a persecuted community. But instead, the word is going out and people are being saved.

To hear that the word of God increased and multiplied in this environment is to be reminded that God is still sovereign even when wicked humans seem to rule the day and to know that his word and his purposes cannot be thwarted (Isa. 55:10–11).

9. We're told explicitly that Herod "did not give God the glory." This sin is easy to recognize in someone who accepts others' worship—but perhaps it's harder to see this same tendency in ourselves. In a blog post called, "Photobombing Jesus—Confessions of a Glory Thief,"[1] Garrett Kell lists six ways we sometimes seek to take God's glory for ourselves.

---

1 Garrett Kell, "Photobombing Jesus—Confessions of a Glory Thief," garrettkell.com, January 19, 2017, http://garrettkell.com/.

- "I want Jesus to be glorified, but I want glory too."
- "Because I want affirmation, I hide my sins."
- "I become bitter when God uses others instead of me."
- "I become more concerned about my public performance than my private devotion."
- "I fear moral failure, mostly because it would defame Jesus, but also because it would defame me."
- "My desire to be something rivals my desire for Jesus to be everything."

Do you recognize some of these things in yourself? Circle the statements you can particularly relate to.

Spend some time in prayer, confessing the ways you fail to give God the glory. Ask Jesus to give you the grace to die to the sin of seeking the glory that belongs to him. Praise him for leaving the glory of heaven and dying a humiliating death, taking upon himself our sin of stealing God's glory. Thank him for coming to save you from seeking your own glory. Cherish the truth that he now dwells in you by his Spirit, empowering you to forsake the sin of stealing his glory.

Discussion Questions

1. When we think or speak about "the hand of the Lord" being on someone, what do you think we usually mean? Is that what we see in this passage?

   We usually mean that God is at work in and through a person in a tangible and visible way to accomplish his purposes. In this passage, the hand of the Lord is with those who are presenting

*the gospel to Gentiles so that a great number of them repent and
believe. But we also see the hand of the Lord at work against
Herod, his enemy, bringing about instantaneous judgment. The
passage speaks to God's intimate involvement with his people,
accomplishing his purposes of salvation and judgment.*

2. Sometimes God works directly, but more often he works
   through means. Through what means do we see the hand of
   the Lord working in this passage?

   *The Lord is at work through the persecution of his people to
   scatter them throughout the world. The Lord is at work through
   the preached word to bring pagan Gentiles to repentance and
   faith. The Lord is at work through his people, such as Barnabas, who brings Saul to Antioch to teach the new believers
   there. The Lord is at work among the new believers, making
   them distinctive so that they are called "Christians." The Lord
   is at work through a prophet, Agabus, to foretell the famine,
   and through the disciples to encourage the believers in Antioch
   to be generous to the believers in Judea. The Lord is at work
   through an angel to lead Peter out of prison (which, you could
   argue, is more direct than through ordinary means). The Lord
   is at work through the prayers of his people to bring Peter out
   of prison safely. The Lord is at work through an angel (again,
   more direct) to strike Herod.*

3. This account of the Gentiles sending relief to their sisters and
   brothers in Judea comes immediately after the story of Peter's
   experience in Caesarea. What do you think it would have been
   like for the Jewish Christians in Judea to receive a financial
   gift from the Gentile Christians in Antioch?

It likely took some time for the Jewish Christians to shift their attitudes toward Gentiles. Receiving a large gift in a time of great need, from someone you had long viewed with skepticism and once thought was far beneath you, would certainly be humbling as well as endearing. Would anything be more powerful in changing your view of people you once despised? This generosity would have accelerated the process of developing family bonds between Christians from people groups that had never before enjoyed positive interaction or close connection.

4. In 12:1, we read about Herod killing the apostle James. This is the first we've heard of James since the twelve apostles were together at Pentecost, which was about ten years earlier. What do you think James has been doing for those ten years? How do you think his murder would have impacted the believers in Jerusalem? (Acts 6:2–4 may give us a clue.)

   In Acts 6:2–4, we read that men were appointed to serve the widows so that the apostles could devote themselves to preaching the word and prayer. Thus we can assume that James has been praying fervently and preaching and teaching the word in and around Jerusalem. The believers would have been heartbroken over his death and praying fervently that the same thing would not happen to Peter (12:5).

5. The believers who have been praying for Peter's release don't believe it's him when he comes to the door. In what ways can you relate to this? Why do you think we struggle to believe that God will really answer our prayers?

Perhaps many of us can relate to earnestly praying for something while having little faith that our prayers will be answered or are being answered. On one hand, this apparent lack of faith may simply reflect the inherent tensions of prayer. We know that God hears our prayers, and that our prayers matter, but we also recognize that his will might not be the same as ours. We know that he will do right, but we don't always know what that right thing is, and so what's ultimately best might not be what we're asking God for. Shadrach, Meshach, and Abednego's response to Nebuchadnezzar provides a good example to us in trusting God even when he does not answer our prayers in the way we might hope: "Our God whom we serve is able to deliver us from the burning fiery furnace, and he will deliver us out of your hand, O king. But if not, be it known to you, O king, that we will not serve your gods or worship the golden image that you have set up" (Dan. 3:17–18).

On the other hand, we may at times pray in unbelief, unconvinced that God hears us. We may doubt his intentions toward us, believing that he doesn't really love us or is withholding good from us. We might doubt his sovereign power to bring about his purposes. Sometimes, though we wouldn't dare admit this even to ourselves, we think the result we're praying toward really requires more human action than divine intervention. So we strategize with human resources rather than truly depend on God to act.

6. We sometimes wonder why God chooses to heal or deliver some from harm but not others. What scriptural truths can we lean into when we are troubled by questions like this?

We tend to want everything to be fair—and we think that we are equipped to determine what is just and fair. In a sense, that was one of Job's complaints against God: that God was not being fair or just toward him in his suffering. When God responded from the whirlwind, one of the questions he asked Job was:

"Will you even put me in the wrong?
  Will you condemn me that you may be in the right?
Have you an arm like God,
    and can you thunder with a voice like his?" (Job 40:8–9)

When God says, "Have you an arm like God?" he's speaking about an arm that executes justice in the world. Job's answer (and our answer) to this question should be, "I don't have the full picture that you have, God, so I can't presume to know what is right and good and fair. But I can trust that you do."

Unless the Lord comes first, we will all face physical death. But for the believer, death is an entryway into eternal life in the presence of Christ. Though we die, we cannot truly perish. Even when God does not protect us from physical suffering or death, we can be sure that he will protect us from eternal suffering and death if we belong to him.

We can lean into truths such as 2 Corinthians 12:9, that the Lord promises to provide sufficient grace for whatever pain he allows in our lives. Or Romans 8:28–29, which tells us that God is so sovereign over suffering that he is able to cause the worst things we can imagine to work together for our good and his glory. Or Romans 8:31–32, which assures us, "If God is for us, who can be against us? He who did not spare his own

Son but gave him up for us all, how will he not also with him graciously give us all things?"

No matter what, if we are joined to Christ by faith, we know that we are in the hands of the one who controls all things, who has the power to bring about his purposes in the world and in our lives. And we know that his purposes are for our good and his glory.

7. Read together Acts 12:23–24. In light of all the events of chapter 12, how do these two verses give us perspective when it seems that evil is winning?

When James was killed, and when Herod was being worshiped as a god, it must have seemed as though the enemies of God's people had the upper hand. But at the end of the chapter, we see Herod experiencing the judgment of God and the word of God increasing and multiplying. We recognize that God's enemies do not have the upper hand. We can always be certain that God is at work accomplishing his purposes in his way and his timing.

Let's close by asking God for the faith to trust him when we don't get what we are praying for, and when it seems like evil is winning in this world and in the lives of those we love.

All That God Had Done with Them

ACTS 13:1–14:28

Personal Bible Study

1. Read Acts 13:1–4. Based on the limited information provided here, what ethnic and religious backgrounds do the five leaders of the Antioch church bring to the table? (See Acts 4:36 and 22:3–5 for additional details.)

   They have racial, ethnic, and religious diversity. They are from Africa, Cyprus, Tarsus, and Judea. Barnabas is a Levite; Paul comes from the Pharisee party. We know Barnabas and Saul are Jewish. We don't know the religious backgrounds of the others, but at least some of them are likely Gentiles. Manaen has a personal connection to Herod.

   According to verse 3 and verse 4, who sends Saul and Barnabas?

   v. 3: *The church does the sending.*

v. 4: *The Holy Spirit does the sending.*

2. Read Acts 13:4–12. This Jewish false prophet and magician calls himself "Bar-Jesus," which means "son of Joshua" or "son of salvation." What is his true identity as revealed by Paul through the Holy Spirit?

   Elymas is a "son of the devil," an "enemy of all righteousness, full of all deceit and villainy." Rather than lead people into salvation, he leads people on a crooked path toward destruction.

   What two things lead to the salvation of the proconsul?

   The divine miracle of judgment in blinding Elymas and the human teaching of Paul and Barnabas.

3. Read Acts 13:13–14. Compare this to 13:5 and 14:1. What do you notice about Paul and Barnabas's strategy as they go from city to city? Why do you think they do this? (Matt. 10:5–6; 15:24; and Rom. 1:16 may help.)

   They first go to the synagogue. They present the offer of salvation first to the Jews and God-fearing Gentiles in the city before offering it more broadly to the Gentiles in the city. "To the Jew first" was the pattern of Jesus's ministry (Matt. 15:24) and his instruction to the apostles (Matt. 10:5–6). While the gospel is intended for all people, chronologically, the gospel message was first revealed to the Jewish people before it was revealed to the Gentiles (non-Jewish people). The ministry of Paul and Barnabas reflects this pattern (Rom. 1:16).

4. Read Acts 13:15–41. The sermon Paul gives in the synagogue in Antioch of Pisidia could be titled "Salvation in Jesus." Provide a summary sentence for each section of his sermon.

vv. 16–25: *Throughout the history of the people of God from Abraham to David, God was providing shadows of his salvation purposes in deliverance from slavery, provision of an inheritance of land, short-term saviors in the era of the judges, and the kingship of David.*

vv. 26–37: *In the life, death, resurrection, and ascension of Jesus, what the prophets wrote about has been fulfilled.*

vv. 38–41: *All who believe in Jesus can experience this salvation of forgiveness and freedom from law-keeping.*

5. Read Acts 13:42–47 and Isaiah 49:5–6. As Paul preaches the message of salvation to "the whole city" (thereby including crowds of Gentiles), the Jews are filled with jealousy. How do Paul and Barnabas use this passage from Isaiah to respond to them?

Paul and Barnabas see themselves as continuing the mission of Jesus, the servant portrayed in Isaiah's "Servant Songs" (see Luke 4:16–21). In Isaiah 49, the servant says that a mission of salvation only to the tribes of Jacob is "too light a thing." The servant's mission, and therefore Paul and Barnabas's mission, is far greater. It is to be a light to all nations—Gentile nations—so that the message of salvation available through faith in Jesus Christ would reach to the end of the earth.

6. Read Acts 13:48–52. How does this passage affirm the significance of both divine election and human response in regard to salvation? How does this reality seem to impact Paul and Barnabas?

Paul and Barnabas present the message of salvation, and those who were appointed for that salvation from before the foundations of the world (Eph. 1:4) respond in faith. Both are required for salvation—divine election and the human response of belief. This seems to free Paul and Barnabas to rejoice. They can be confident that their labor really matters: God has used their presentation of the gospel to draw many to faith! But they need not feel that they have failed when others refuse to believe. They can rest in knowing that the gospel saves some and hardens others.

7. Read Acts 14:1–7. Paul and Barnabas are met with murderous opposition in Iconium. What can we learn from their response?

They are criticized and lied about by the unbelieving Jews, but they don't leave because of that. They remain for a long time, continuing to bear witness to the grace of Jesus to those who will listen and healing people by the power of the Spirit. They are not in a rush to leave because they want to build up these new believers as long as possible in spite of the opposition. Then when plans for their murder come to light, they leave. Yet even when they flee, they don't go silent. They continue preaching the gospel. Opposition changes their location and audience, but it does not fundamentally change their mission or commitment to preach the word.

8. Read Acts 14:8–18. How is Paul's "sermon" to the Gentiles in Lystra different from his sermon to the Jews and God-fearing Gentiles in Antioch of Pisidia (Acts 13:16–41)? How is it similar?

Paul's sermon to the Jews and God-fearing Gentiles in Pisidian Antioch is based on the Old Testament, showing that Jesus was the fulfillment of what was written. When speaking to the pagan Gentiles in Lystra, however, Paul doesn't begin with Jewish history or quote Scripture, both of which would be meaningless to them. Instead, he begins where they are, pointing to truths that are evident and accessible to them. Paul appeals to their experi-

ence of creation, showing that it was created by the one true God who is worthy of their worship. In both cases, he frames his message as "good news." Both sermons urge the listener to turn, or repent, and put their faith in God and the Savior he has sent.

9. Read Acts 14:19–26. On the map below, trace the path Paul and Barnabas have taken so far in this first missionary journey (13:1–14:20) from Antioch to Seleucia, to Salamis, to Paphos, to Perga in Pamphylia, to Antioch in Pisidia, to Iconium, to Lysta, and to Derbe. Then trace the path they take back to Antioch.

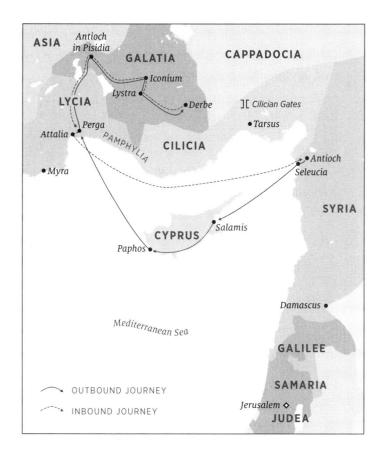

Why do you think they do not take the more direct land route from Derbe to Antioch of Syria?

They are not concerned to get back to Antioch as much as they are concerned to strengthen the believers and develop the churches they have planted. They revisit all the cities where they have invested time and seen people come to believe in Christ—even the ones where they were persecuted. These brand-new churches full of brand-new believers would have had so much immaturity and ignorance, such need for guidance and encouragement and good teaching. Paul and Barnabas want to strengthen them for the certain difficulties that are part of belonging to Christ's kingdom. They also work to appoint elders who can lead these churches well.

10. Read Acts 14:24–27. In question 1, you were asked who sent Paul and Barnabas. Similarly, who did the work according to these final verses?

Paul and Barnabas fulfilled the work that the church commended them to accomplish, and they declared "all that God had done with them." Clearly they worked at proclaiming, teaching, discipling, traveling, enduring, praying, and encouraging. But they recognize that their work was empowered by the grace of God at work in them and through them. It was the Lord who "opened a door of faith to the Gentiles," and ultimately he receives the glory for what was accomplished.

11. In this passage we see Paul and Barnabas experience murderous opposition. Yet we also see them return to places where they faced opposition in their mission to serve and strengthen the

church. How does their example challenge or encourage you as you think about facing opposition or prioritizing service to the church?

Personal response.

Discussion Questions

1. Have you ever expressed appreciation to someone for her ministry, and her response was, "Oh, it wasn't me, it was the Lord"—or have you said something similar yourself when recognized or thanked? What are the pros and cons of this type of response? What are some other ways we could respond?

   Often this kind of response comes from a genuine desire for humility. We really do sense that the Spirit is the one who empowered and enabled us, and it's good that we want the Lord to receive the glory. At the same time, our discomfort with praise or encouragement can in some sense diminish his glory. If we deflect compliments, we may inadvertently minimize the Spirit's work in equipping and empowering us. In his sovereign wisdom, he did not simply accomplish the task miraculously—he chose to work through human means. Acknowledging the role of obedience, faithfulness, or hard work can be a different form of evidence that the Holy Spirit is at work in us. Additionally, recognizing and valuing a person's hard work or faithful sowing can challenge or inspire others to similar God-honoring effort.

   Perhaps when we're recognized or thanked, we could consider responding in a way that acknowledges this tension between the Spirit's work and human effort. It could be as simple as,

"Thank you! Isn't God good?" "I love getting to participate in what the Lord is doing." "I'm grateful God chooses to work through humans like me!" "I'm so glad it was helpful. I couldn't have done it without the power of the Spirit at work in me." (These examples aren't meant to serve as a list of "approved" responses, of course, but merely some ideas to get you thinking about how to receive encouragement with humility, in a way that reflects both the Spirit's work and human effort.)

2. Nancy said that Barnabas and Saul set off to fulfill a divine plan using human strategy. How would you describe the divine plan? And what elements are likely part of their human strategy?

    The divine plan is to fulfill Isaiah 49:6 and Acts 1:8, taking the gospel of salvation through Jesus to the end of the earth. It is for Saul to fulfill his God-appointed role—that of the apostle to the Gentiles. The human strategy is for a team to travel to major cities. They present the offer of salvation first to the Jews and God-fearing Gentiles in the city before offering it more broadly to the Gentiles in the city. Barnabas and Saul stay in the cities long enough to establish churches and then visit them again later, if possible, to strengthen them by appointing elders. Paul also writes to the churches to correct and encourage them. As the churches in major cities are established and grow, they become sending churches to reach the region around them.

3. At the first stop on their first missionary journey in Salamis, the Roman proconsul believes the gospel, and a Jewish magician experiences divine judgment. How do you think this would

have impacted both Jews and Gentiles in this city? (Note especially what Paul says to Elymas in 13:10.)

The Jews would have been shocked and likely offended to hear Paul say that this Jewish "son of Abraham" was really a "son of the devil." They would have also been provoked and challenged that this one who called himself a "son of salvation" was actually hindering people from finding salvation. They would likely have been shocked that this high-profile Jew, who seemed to have supernatural power, experienced immediate divine judgment by being made blind for a time.

The Gentiles would have been shocked that their Roman leader put his faith in the Jewish Messiah. We don't know, but we could imagine that many things may have changed in the way he exercised his power in the city after his conversion.

Both groups may have been surprised to have traditional categories upended—to learn that Jews could be outsiders and Gentiles could be the ones who have genuine faith and are welcomed in.

4. How do we see both divine election and human response at work in Acts 13:48–52?

Paul and Barnabas present the message of salvation, and those who were appointed for that salvation from "before the foundation of the world" (Eph. 1:4) respond in faith. Both are required for salvation—divine election and the human response of belief. This seems to free Paul and Barnabas to rejoice. They can be confident that their labor really matters: God uses their presentation of the gospel to draw many to faith.

But they need not feel that they have failed when many refuse to believe. They can rest in knowing that the gospel saves some and hardens others.

5. While we should always be prepared and take the opportunities God gives us to present Christ, we don't have to feel like failures when someone responds with apathy, indignation, or outright rejection. It's simply not all up to us. How does this encourage or challenge you as you think about sharing the gospel?

   Personal response.

6. How is Paul's "sermon" to the Gentiles in Lystra (14:8–18) different from his sermon to the Jews and God-fearing Gentiles in Antioch in Pisidia (Acts 13:16–41)? How does this challenge you as you think about sharing Christ in different situations with different types of people?

   Paul's sermon to the Jews and God-fearing Gentiles in Antioch in Pisidia was based on the Old Testament writings and prophets, showing that Jesus was the fulfillment of what was written. For his message to the pagan Gentiles in Lystra, he appeals to their experience of creation, presenting it as created by the one true God who is worthy of their worship. The messages are similar in that both appeal to the listener to turn or repent and put their faith in God and the Savior he has sent.

   This challenges us to carefully consider the understanding and assumptions of our listeners when we're presenting the gospel. It challenges us to do our homework, to know people well enough that we're able to start from where they are and share the gospel in a way that connects with their lived experience. And it frees us to approach different types of people and different situations in different ways, recognizing that our gospel presentation doesn't always have to sound the same.

7. Nancy said, "So often people think that if God will just do a miracle, then people will believe. But miracles don't always lead to genuine faith. They can lead to complete confusion." Why are miracles inadequate? What has God given us that leads to genuine faith?

Miracles of healing do not provide objective truth. They are subject to interpretation and can easily be misinterpreted. What we need for genuine faith is divine revelation, which we have in the Bible. The Spirit uses the read and preached word to generate genuine faith, as Paul wrote to the Romans: "Faith comes from hearing, and hearing through the word of Christ" (Rom 10:17).

8. How do we see both the Holy Spirit at work and humans working in this section of Acts? What implications does this have for our own ministry efforts?

In 13:3–4 we're told that the church sends Barnabas and Paul and that the Holy Spirit does the sending. Similarly, when Paul and Barnabas return to Antioch, their efforts are described as "work that they had fulfilled" (14:26). Yet they declared "all that God had done with them, and how he had opened a door of faith to the Gentiles" (14:27). Paul and Barnabas clearly worked at proclaiming, teaching, discipling, traveling, enduring, praying, and encouraging. At the same time, they recognized that the grace of God was at work in them and through them, and ultimately, they gave God the glory for what was accomplished.

We see this pattern referenced repeatedly in Paul's epistles. In Colossians 1:29, Paul says, "I toil, struggling with all his energy that he powerfully works within me." He tells the Philippian church to "work out your own salvation with fear and trembling, for it is God who works in you" (Phil. 2:12–13). Our calling is the same today: we commit to hard work, giving ourselves to proclaiming, teaching, discipling, traveling, enduring, praying, and encouraging people. And as we work, we trust that God will work in and through us to accomplish his salvation purposes.

Let's close by thanking God for his willingness to work in and through us, and by offering ourselves to him to be used for his purposes in the world.

Lesson 11

Saved through the Grace
of the Lord Jesus

ACTS 15:1–16:5

Personal Bible Study

1. Read Acts 15:1–2. How is this prerequisite for salvation different from what Peter and Paul have preached? (For help see 2:38; 3:19–20; 10:43; 13:38–39.)

   Peter and Paul have preached that repentance and faith, or belief in Jesus, is required. They usually instruct baptism as a mark of repentance and faith. The men from Judea (or Jerusalem) are saying that circumcision is required. In essence, they are saying that Gentiles must become Jews first to be Christians and thereby must follow the laws of Moses.

2. Read Acts 15:3–5. What types of things would the Gentiles be required to do to "keep the law of Moses"? (Gal. 6:12 and Col. 2:16–17 may help.)

In addition to males being circumcised, Gentiles would be required to keep the food laws and observe the Jewish calendar, which would include making trips to the temple in Jerusalem and offering sacrifices.

3. Read Acts 15:6–11. Summarize Peter's argument in each of the following verses:

   v. 7: *God called him to declare the gospel to the Gentiles.*

   v. 8: *God gave the Holy Spirit to Gentile believers just like he did to Jewish believers.*

   v. 9: *God made no distinction between Jews and Gentiles. He cleanses the hearts of both by faith (rather than by circumcision).*

   v. 10: *The Jews could never keep the law of Moses, so why should they put the burden of trying to keep the law on the Gentiles?*

   v. 11: *Jews are saved through the grace of Jesus just like Gentiles are.*

4. Read Acts 15:12. How does Paul and Barnabas's testimony of the signs and wonders God performed through them support Peter's argument?

   The fact that God did signs and wonders through Paul and Barnabas among the Gentiles indicates that God is at work among the Gentiles for their salvation.

5. Read Acts 15:13–18, where James quotes Amos 9:11–12. What do you think it means that "the tent of David . . . has fallen"? (See 1 Kings 12:16–17.)

The kingdom under David's descendant Rehoboam was divided into the northern and southern kingdoms of Israel and Judah.

Toward what end will the Lord rebuild and restore "the tent of David"?

His purpose is that "the remnant of mankind," or "all the Gentiles" called by the Lord's name, would be able to seek him and become a part of his people.

6. Read Acts 15:19–21. Why do you think the apostles and elders in Jerusalem determine that the new Gentile believers should abstain from the things listed in verse 20? (This is rather challenging to discern confidently from the text, so do your best. It will be clarified in the chapter or video session.)

   These things are all closely identified with pagan idol worship; as such, they are particularly offensive to Jews. The Gentiles should turn away from these things as part of making a clean break with their old lives of pagan idolatry. Because the Jews are still immersed in the law of Moses, abstaining from these things will keep the Gentiles from offending their Jewish brothers and sisters as well as Jews who have not yet come to faith.

7. Read Acts 15:22–35. Why do you think the Jewish and Gentile believers in the Antioch church would have rejoiced and been encouraged and strengthened by the contingent from the Jerusalem church?

   After the dissension caused by the demands made by the men from the Jerusalem church, the Jews and Gentiles in the Antioch church likely would have felt relief and joy in a peaceful resolution. They would have been helped and strengthened by the clarity of this definitive decision from the apostles at the "mother" church. They are encouraged and strengthened in their faith as Barsabbas and Silas preach the word to them.

8. Read Acts 15:36–41. Chapter 15 began with a disagreement regarding whether Gentiles should be circumcised that caused "no small dissension and debate." In these final verses, there is a "sharp disagreement" regarding ministry staffing. The earlier disagreement was a gospel issue. Do you think this disagreement has the same significance? Why or why not?

The earlier disagreement was over a matter essential to how a person is saved and made right with God. It was a first-order issue that had to be clarified for the gospel to continue to go out faithfully. The disagreement in verses 36–41 is not over an issue that threatens the substance of the gospel; rather, it's a matter of strategy or staffing.

In what way is the outcome of both disagreements similar? (See v. 32 and v. 41.)

The outcome of the two disagreements is similar in that both result in the church being strengthened.

9. Read Acts 16:1–5. In chapter 15, Paul argued against circumcision as a requirement for Gentiles. Why do you think he now wants Timothy, a Gentile believer, to be circumcised? (Once again, this may be rather challenging to discern confidently from the text, so do your best. It will be clarified in the chapter or video session. Paul's approach to ministry as expressed in 1 Cor. 9:19–23 may be helpful.)

Paul's strategy in every city is to go first to the Jews, seeking them out at the local synagogue. Paul recognizes that the Jews will likely be unwilling to listen to the message of the gospel presented by Timothy if he remains uncircumcised. Taken together, these two chapters tell us that if someone is demanding circumcision as a prerequisite to salvation, Paul will stand firm against it. But if circumcision will enhance the possibility of a hearing for the gospel, he's all for it. His approach is to "become all things to all people, that by all means I might save some" (1 Cor. 9:22).

What does this passage reveal as the continuing fruit of the conflict in Jerusalem, Paul and Barnabas's conflict, and Paul's request of Timothy?

The churches are strengthened in the faith and increasing in numbers.

10. This passage has covered two disagreements and a significant decision that are all fraught with conflict. Conflict in the church can be incredibly painful, disillusioning, and disappointing. What do you think it looks like to work through conflict in a way that strengthens the church and advances the gospel?

To work through conflict, we must align our priorities with the ones reflected here. Rather than operating from a desire to win arguments or advance personal preferences, we must prioritize in our own hearts the strengthening of the church and the advance of the gospel. Believers involved in conflict can learn from and emulate the posture and actions of the church leaders in this passage: they look to Scripture (15:15–18) and seek the Holy Spirit's guidance (15:28); they humbly recognize that everyone is saved by the grace of the Lord Jesus alone (15:11); they value the conversion of unbelievers as a source of joy (15:3), speaking of and celebrating what God has done (15:4); and they are so committed to the spread of the gospel that they make sacrifices to remove any stumbling block that would hinder people from hearing this good news (16:3).

Ephesians 4:1–3 describes what it looks like to walk "in a manner worthy of the calling to which you have been called": as we navigate conflict, we are called to conduct ourselves "with all humility and gentleness, with patience, bearing with one another in love, eager to maintain the unity of the Spirit in the bond of peace." Walking in this manner requires that we bear with those who have preferences and positions different from our own, refusing to assume the worst of them, refusing to give in to cynicism, gossip, harsh talk, or arrogant assumptions.

Discussion Questions

1. In what way(s) does the disagreement regarding requiring Gentiles to become Jews before becoming Christians threaten the spread of the gospel?

   If the gospel going out to the world requires following the Mosaic ceremonial law, it is not the true gospel of salvation by grace alone through faith alone. If Gentiles are told they have to become Jews first in order to become Christians, not only will it create a significant hurdle for Gentiles; it will also betray the truth that "a person is not justified by works of the law but through faith in Jesus Christ . . . because by works of the law no one will be justified" (Gal. 2:16). Paul is firm in his rebuke to the Galatian church about this: "If righteousness were through the law, then Christ died for no purpose" (Gal. 2:21). Adding requirements about diet, circumcision, and temple sacrifices to the gospel effectively renders Christ's sacrifice insufficient, falsely implying that we can add something to the righteousness he alone provides.

2. Peter says in 15:11, "But we believe *we* will be saved through the grace of the Lord Jesus, just as *they* will." Notice that even though they are discussing how Gentiles will be saved, he doesn't say, "But we believe *they* will be saved through the grace of the Lord Jesus just as *we* will." Why might that wording make a difference?

   Perhaps it emphasizes to them as Jewish Christians the nature of their own salvation. After a life defined by the law of Moses, they probably need frequent reminders that they aren't saved through law-keeping, but have been saved by grace. This might help them to see that the Gentiles also cannot be saved through law-keeping, but only by grace.

3. How are the Jewish and Gentile believers in the Antioch church encouraged and strengthened by the contingent from the Jerusalem church?

   They are glad to know that they do not need to labor under an impossible burden. Perhaps they also rejoice to feel cared for and shepherded by the apostles in Jerusalem. The apostles' clear, definitive decision provides clarity and confidence to the Antioch church going forward.

4. What does Colossians 4:10 (written many years after the events of Acts 15) reveal about the dispute between Paul, Mark, and

Barnabas? How does that encourage you regarding church conflict you have experienced in the past or are experiencing in the present?

Mark is with Paul while he is under house arrest in Rome, and Paul instructs the church in Colossae to welcome Barnabas. Clearly the dispute has been put behind them, and there has been reconciliation and redemption.

5. Timothy willingly submits to circumcision for the sake of helping Jews hear the gospel. Why do we bristle at the idea of giving up our freedoms for the cause of the gospel? What are some examples today of freedoms that believers can enjoy but might be wise to sacrifice for the sake of loving others and enabling them to hear the gospel?

   We bristle at giving up our freedoms for the cause of the gospel because we are often selfish. We absorb our culture's mindset of demanding our rights. Perhaps our clinging tightly to our rights reflects a lack of valuing the eternal inheritance that can never be taken from us.

   In some cases, we might be blind to the ways that clinging to our freedoms can be a stumbling block for others. Or perhaps we lack love for Christ and others. We simply aren't deeply concerned for others' salvation or committed to the spread of the gospel. We don't see Jesus as a treasure worth giving up everything else to gain, or to help others gain.

   Note: Many specific freedoms could be listed here; your group will likely come up with various examples based on their own experiences and perspectives. Challenge group members to think about freedoms they enjoy and might have a hard time giving up, not just freedoms "other believers" should give up. It's easy to point at what others should sacrifice, but what might we choose to lay down in order to help others hear the gospel?

6. In Acts 15:32; 15:41; and 16:5 we read that the churches are being strengthened, even though they're dealing with conflict. In what ways do you think working through conflict constructively can strengthen churches?

The church in Antioch is strengthened as the conflict over circumcision leads to greater clarity about the gospel—requirements for salvation and priorities for those who have been saved. The churches in Syria and Cilicia are strengthened by the ministry of Paul and Silas, who persevere in the mission even after the conflict with Barnabas and Mark. The churches in Galatia are strengthened in faith and in number by the same clarity about the gospel and its demands as Paul, Silas, and Timothy come to minister to them.

Conflict over doctrine forces people to get clear on what they believe and why. It raises a decision point: What exactly does this Scripture mean? What are the implications of it? And how important is this—is it central to the gospel or is it secondary? Can we "agree to disagree," or must we part ways over this? As believers work through these questions, the end result can be greater unity and greater confidence in what they believe. If a parting of ways is required, those who remain are united by their common convictions. If the issue is determined to be of secondary importance, believers who disagree can strengthen their commitment to the core truths of the gospel and grow in mutual respect and patience for those who see its outworking differently. Or perhaps as people discuss their disagreements, some are persuaded to change their positions and align more closely with Scripture (as we'll see when Priscilla and Aquila help Apollos to understand "the way of God more accurately" in Acts 18:26).

We so often think of conflict as a bad thing. But it doesn't have to be, if the parties involved proceed with love, respect, and a commitment to the glory of Jesus Christ as they work through their differences. The process of disagreeing and coming together to work through it can make relationships stronger. And even if separation over a secondary issue seems necessary, a peaceful separation can actually multiply the spread of the gospel as believers head in different directions.

7. In this passage we covered a dispute about salvation requirements for Gentiles, a disagreement about ministry staffing, and a decision about how a disciple uses his or her freedom. What priorities guide how the early church works through each of these issues?

   Dispute about salvation requirements for Gentiles: *Peter appeals to what God has done through him among the Gentiles and how the Holy Spirit has worked among them. He puts a priority on not burdening the Gentiles with something the Jews had never been able to live out. Most importantly, he centers his argument on the core truth of the gospel: salvation is by grace alone, through faith alone. James appeals to Scripture to demonstrate how the salvation of Gentiles was always a part of God's plan.*

Disagreement about ministry staffing: *Paul prioritizes proven faithfulness. Barnabas prioritizes grace after failure. Neither man lets the difference in priorities hinder him from advancing the gospel.*

Decision about how a disciple uses his or her freedom: *In Paul's asking Timothy to be circumcised and in Timothy's submission to circumcision, both men prioritize love for the lost and removing obstacles to enable the gospel to be heard.*

8. If you have been in the church for any length of time, you have likely experienced conflict. Church conflict often creates its own kind of hurt that can be hard to overcome. What do you think it looks like to walk through church conflict "in a manner worthy of the calling to which you have been called, with all humility and gentleness, with patience, bearing with one another in love, eager to maintain the unity of the Spirit in the bond of peace," as Ephesians 4:1–3 describes?

It looks like being more committed to unity and peace than to getting my own way or proving that I was right. It requires that we bear with those who have preferences and positions that are opposed to our own, refusing to assume the worst of them, refusing to give in to cynicism, gossip, harsh talk, or arrogant assumptions.

But this doesn't mean that we ignore real problems that need to be addressed. It often means that we are willing to have hard conversations rather than avoiding or ignoring tensions or disagreements. We can and should speak up and raise issues that need to be addressed. Out of love for Christ and his church, we want to be sure to do so with a spirit of humility, toward the aim that God would be glorified by our genuine love, gospel clarity, and biblical faithfulness.

Let's close by asking God to give us the wisdom and the will to lay down our freedoms for the cause of the gospel. Let's also ask him for the wisdom and grace to navigate conflict in the church in a way that will bring him great glory and bless the church.

Lesson 12

There Is Another King, Jesus

ACTS 16:6–17:9

Personal Bible Study

1. Read Acts 16:6–12. How do these verses demonstrate that
   Jesus is directing the spread of his gospel to the nations?

   *Jesus works through the Holy Spirit, who blocks Paul and Silas's
   path twice, forbidding them to speak the word in Asia and not
   allowing them to go into Bithynia. When Paul sees the vision
   of the man of Macedonia urging him to come, he recognizes
   it as the call of God to go to Macedonia, and he immediately
   charts a course to go there.*

   When Paul sees a vision of a Macedonian man saying, "Come . . .
   help us" (16:9), what does he conclude is the best way to "help"?

He concludes that God has called them "to preach the gospel" in Macedonia. All of Paul's subsequent actions in this passage revolve around preaching Jesus Christ as the help everyone needs most. Paul speaks to the women at the place of prayer (16:13), commands the spirit to come out of the slave girl "in the name of Jesus Christ" (16:18), invites the jailer to "believe in the Lord Jesus" (16:31), and explains and proves in the Thessalonian synagogue that Jesus is the Christ (17:2–3).

2. Read Acts 16:13–15. So far in Acts we've witnessed many supernatural events. What supernatural activity do you see in these verses?

"The Lord opened [Lydia's] heart to pay attention to what was said by Paul." Apart from a supernatural work of the Holy Spirit, no one opens her heart to the gospel. The natural heart is hard, deceived, and wicked. Only a heart supernaturally made new by the Spirit can be moved to repentance and faith.

What actions does Lydia take in response to the gospel?

Lydia and her household are baptized, and then she urges Paul and his companions to come stay at her house.

3. Read Acts 16:16–18 and Luke 8:27–29. What similarities do you see? How does Matthew 12:22–29 help to explain what happens in Acts?

The demons recognize Jesus as the Son of the Most High God in Luke, and they recognize Paul and his companions as servants of the Most High God in Acts. Jesus commands the demons to depart and go to the pigs, and they do. Paul commands the demons to come out of the slave girl in the name of Jesus, and they do.

The Matthew passage helps to explain that Jesus and Paul had power to tell the demons to depart because Jesus has bound up the "strong man," Satan. Paul's casting out of demons indicates that the kingdom of Jesus has come upon the people of Philippi.

4. Read Acts 16:19–27. What are Paul and Silas doing in prison? What impact do you think this might have had on those around them?

   Despite their tremendous physical suffering, Paul and Silas are praying and singing hymns to God, worshiping late into the night. The text says that the other "prisoners were listening to them" (v. 25)—surely it would have been shocking to see wounded men in chains full of joy and peace and hope.

5. Read Acts 16:28–34. How is the jailer's response to the word of the Lord similar to Lydia's response in verse 15?

   The jailer believes and is baptized along with all his family. He takes Paul and Silas into his house, washes their wounds, and feeds them. And he rejoices! Both he and Lydia immediately extend hospitality as a response to hearing the gospel.

6. Read Acts 16:35–40. Why do you think Paul announces that he and Silas are Roman citizens and refuses to leave secretly?

   According to the ESV Study Bible, it was illegal under Roman law to scourge or imprison a Roman citizen without a formal hearing.[1] *Paul's announcement that they are Roman citizens would highlight the injustice of their treatment. They are not criminals; they have been mistreated by officials who have broken the law. Paul and Silas want the message of Jesus and the reputation of his followers to be honorable. Public vindication would help prevent the gospel and the new community of believers from being associated with criminal activity.*

7. Read Acts 17:1–9. In what ways are the charges against the believers true?

Paul and Silas are indeed saying that "there is another king, Jesus" (v. 7). And Jesus is the opposite of Caesar in every way. Rather than a human king who claimed to be a god, Jesus was God who became human. Rather than demand to be worshiped and served, Jesus came in humility to serve and even lay down his life for his people. And rather than Caesar who reigned on a limited area of the earth for only a few years, Jesus is an eternal king who reigns over all the universe.

Paul and Silas are not acting against the decrees of Caesar in terms of encouraging disobedience to Caesar's government. Jesus taught that his kingdom was not of this world (John 18:36). Allegiance to Jesus as king dictates that we be subject to human authorities instituted by God, unless those authorities demand that we disobey God. Yet in some sense, it's true that the kingdom Paul and Silas proclaim is a threat to Caesar's kingdom simply because Caesar demands to be

---

1 *ESV Study Bible*, ed. Wayne Grudem (Wheaton, IL: Crossway, 2008), note on Acts 16:37.

worshiped. Embracing Jesus as king means acknowledging that no one is worthy of worship but Jesus alone.

8. Work your way back through 16:6–17:9 and trace the action on the map below by drawing in the path taken by Paul, Silas, and Timothy (and Luke himself for some of it).

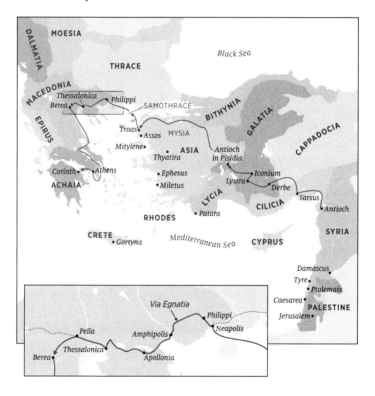

9. How has King Jesus turned your world upside down so that your life reflects his kingdom values? In what ways do your values or priorities need to shift so that they align with his kingdom?

Personal response.

Discussion Questions

1. Have you ever made ministry plans that you were sure God would bless but then been prevented from carrying them out? How does this account of the Spirit's forbidding Paul and Silas's ministry plans help you think about your own thwarted ministry plans?

   We know that Paul did later go to Asia (Ephesus), and that Peter wrote to Christians living in Bithynia (1 Pet. 1:1), so the gospel did eventually go to those places. Sometimes it may be that our plans are not bad but that the work needs to be done at another time, or in another way, or by someone else. King Jesus is in charge of the spread of his gospel, and we know that all of his plans are wise and good. So when our plans are thwarted, we might feel disappointed, but we can trust in God's sovereignty over those plans.

2. We might wish that God would give us visions that tell us exactly what to do, like he gave Paul. But how does God provide us with the guidance we need for ministry decisions?

   God, in his sovereignty and providence, is able to turn our hearts and minds to achieve his plans for us (Prov. 16:9; 21:1). He gives us wise counsel through other trusted believers (Prov. 11:14; 24:6). He can always speak to his people and guide them with their conscious cooperation. However, we cannot draw the conclusion that God will guide us in the same way today as he guided a few specific people in redemptive history.

   As those who have always had access to Scripture, we could easily lose sight of how remarkable it is that God has spoken to us by his Son (Heb. 1:1–2) and through his word (1 Thess. 2:13; Heb. 3:7–9). We have the whole of the Old and New Testaments that provide us with godly wisdom and guidance. As we read the Bible or hear it taught, we hear the voice of God telling us what we most need to know. Through the work of the Spirit applying the word to our hearts, he awakens a response in us and leads us to follow him. We might wish for something more mystical or magical, but it is actually extraordinary that the living God speaks to us in this way.

Some may say, "I'm waiting for the Lord's leading" about a decision, as if they are expecting God to impart fresh revelations to them above and beyond Scripture. But nowhere in Scripture are we urged to seek signs, visions, dreams, or still, small voices. Rather, we are urged to study and meditate on Scripture as the very words of God and expect that God, by his Spirit, will give us the wisdom we need. We are free to serve God rightly without fear, and free of the tyranny of trying to discern his will through feelings of peace or by interpreting the circumstances of life, which can often be ambiguous.

3. Nancy proposed the possibility that Paul and Silas were singing Psalm 119, specifically verses 61–62, while suffering in prison. What other psalms do you think would have been helpful in their circumstances? Are there certain psalms you find comforting to read or sing when you are suffering? What do you think it would have been like for the other prisoners and the jailer to hear their singing?

Personal response. Other ideas might include Psalms 23; 69; 71; 121; or 149.

It must have been stunning and perhaps confusing to the other prisoners and the jailer to hear Paul and Silas singing from a prison cell. Perhaps it made them curious to know this God who inspired Paul and Silas to have such confident hope.

4. Have you ever experienced what seemed like supernatural joy or peace in the worst of circumstances? Or have you known someone else who did? What is the effect of seeing someone demonstrate steadfast faith in Christ while suffering?

   Personal response.

5. Nancy suggested that when the jailer asked, "Sirs, what must I do to be saved?" he may not have been seeking spiritual salvation. If that is the case, in what way did he get much more than he even knew to ask for?

   Not only was he saved from taking his own life or having his life taken from him, if his prisoners had escaped, but he was also given eternal life in Christ. And not just him, but his whole family. He went from despair to rejoicing.

6. The mob in Thessalonica accused Paul and Silas of turning the world upside down. Think about what it was like to live under the kingdom of Rome and Caesar. In what ways did Paul and Silas's message of the kingdom of Jesus truly "turn the world upside down"? (For insights about Jesus's kingdom, consider reading Matt. 5:1–12; Luke 9:46–48; 18:17, 24; John 18:36.)

   Paul and Silas called people to come under the rule of King Jesus, who was a very different kind of king from Caesar. Jesus was not a human king who claimed to be a god. He was God who became human. Rather than demand to be worshiped and served, he came in humility to serve and even lay down his life for his people. And rather than Caesar who reigned on a limited area of the earth for only a few years, Jesus is an eternal king who reigns over all the universe.

Presenting Jesus as king and calling people to come into his kingdom did not mean they were acting against the decrees of Caesar. While Jesus demands our highest loyalty, because his kingdom is not of this world, our allegiance to King Jesus requires that we be subject to human authorities instituted by God unless those authorities demand that we disobey God. So Paul and Silas were not "turning the world upside down" in terms of a political revolution, as the mob accused. Rather, they were advocating a whole new set of values, a way to live under the rule of Caesar as a citizen of God's kingdom. And as more and more people embraced Jesus as their ultimate king, it would have a transforming effect on the culture in a way that would indeed turn the world upside down.

Their lives of worshiping the Roman gods and the Roman rulers would have been turned upside down. Their lives of being enslaved to sin would have been turned upside down as they lived out obedience to God. Those who had power would no longer lord it over their subjects, but would lead and serve with humility. Those seen by society as least in value or status would be treated with dignity. Wealth would not be hoarded or spent selfishly but shared generously, believing that it was not lost but being stored up in heaven.

7. How has the gospel of Jesus Christ continued to turn the world upside down in the two thousand years since Paul and Silas

preached? What values does the kingdom of God proclaim that are the opposite of what our society values today? How does the kingdom of God challenge your own priorities and values?

Personal response.

Let's close by praying for God's kingdom to come in all of its "upside down" power to our world, our country, our city, our church, our families, and in our own lives.

Lesson 13

I Have Many in This City
Who Are My People

ACTS 17:10–18:23

Personal Bible Study

1. Read Acts 17:10–15. How does the response of the Bereans set a pattern and provide encouragement for all believers?

   They receive the word of God with eagerness. But they don't just take Paul and Silas's word for it—they "examined the Scriptures daily to see if these things were so." They take God's word seriously and weigh what these new teachers proclaim against the truth of Scripture. And this leads to belief! We can be encouraged knowing that the Bible can be understood rightly by ordinary people who approach it with openness, receptivity, willingness to think carefully, and dependence on the Holy Spirit.

2. Read Acts 17:16–21. What is Paul's emotional response to what he encounters in Athens? How does he respond practically?

Paul is "provoked," or troubled, by the idolatry of the city, represented by its temples, altars, and statues. Perhaps we could say he is grieved at how lost and deceived the people are or filled with righteous anger that the Athenians are giving glory to idols instead of the one true and living God. Practically, rather than condemn or withdraw, Paul engages with the Athenians. He reasons with the Jews and God-fearing Gentiles in the synagogue, converses with the philosophers in the marketplace, and makes his case for the one true God before the Areopagus.

3. Read Acts 17:22–34. To what does Paul appeal in the Areopagus? How is that different from the basis of his appeal in the synagogue?

Paul appeals to their religious impulses. He begins where they are and uses the observable truth of creation, as well as the insights of their own poets, to point them to Jesus Christ. This is different from his appeals in the synagogue, where he begins with Scripture that the Jews know and trust and reasons from there to show how Jesus fulfills it.

What does Paul communicate about the purpose God is working out in history in verses 26–27?

God has arranged people and nations and time periods for the purpose of people seeking him and finding him.

What is the implication of the first coming and promised return of Jesus for all people according to verses 30–31?

Be ready to face judgment, because Jesus will return to judge all unrighteousness. God has so far withheld the judgment that is deserved. Since Christ has come, died, risen, and ascended into heaven, we are now in the period of redemptive history await-ing his return. While Jesus came the first time to accomplish and offer salvation, he will come the second time to judge the world in righteousness. All people are commanded to repent and thereby be preserved in the judgment.

4. Read Acts 18:1–6 along with Luke 9:5. How do these two passages relate? What is being communicated by the actions described?

   Paul is following Jesus's instructions to his disciples that as you proclaim the kingdom of God, if people do not receive you, you should "shake off the dust from your feet as a testi-mony against them." This is a visible illustration of giving over to judgment those who refuse the message of Christ's messengers. It indicates that the messenger has faithfully presented the word of God and that those who have rejected it are responsible for their failure to receive it and respond in repentance.

5. Read Acts 18:7–8. The Jews who rejected Paul's message could not have been very happy with the developments in these verses. What things are likely bothersome to them?

   The new believers begin to meet in Titius Justus's home, which is right next door to the synagogue. The growth of the church would be right in their face all the time. In addition, Crispus, the ruler of the synagogue, is one of those who begin worshiping with the church next door.

6. Read Acts 18:9–10 with John 10:16 and Ephesians 1:3–4. In what ways would the words of Jesus that Paul heard in his vision have emboldened him to take the gospel further into the pagan city of Corinth?

   Paul would have been encouraged to know that the Lord's presence would be with him and would protect him from harm. He would have been assured that God was going to use his proclamation of the gospel to save those who from eternity past had been chosen in Christ for salvation. He could rest in knowing that God would work by his Spirit, drawing to himself those who belonged to him.

7. Read Acts 18:11–17. How is the Lord's promise to Paul in his vision fulfilled in these events?

   Over eighteen months, Paul is "not . . . silent" (v. 9), but is able to teach the word of God among the Corinthians, persuading those who are "[the Lord's] people" to take hold of Christ (v. 10). When he is brought before the tribunal, the ruling authority rejects the charges against him, so he is protected from conviction, punishment, and perhaps being put out of the city. Paul is able to continue ministering in Corinth without fear. Because Gallio's ruling establishes legal precedent that Christianity is a sect of the Jewish religion, an approved religion, and thereby protected under Roman law, it provides protection more broadly to believers throughout the Roman Empire over the next ten years.

8. Read Acts 18:18–23. Go back to the map in lesson 12 and draw arrows to complete the route of Paul's second missionary journey. (When we read in v. 22 that Paul "went up and

greeted the church," he is most likely speaking of going up to Jerusalem, which was at a higher elevation than Caesarea.)

9. Everywhere Paul goes, rather than condemn, criticize, or ignore, Paul engages with people who see the world differently than he does and who have no hope in Christ. What do you think is your default mindset when it comes to interaction with the culture and systems around you where Christ is not honored? What could it look like for you to thoughtfully engage instead of condemn, criticize, or ignore?

Personal response.

Discussion Questions

1. The Jews in Berea are "examining the Scriptures daily" (17:11) to see if what Paul is saying is so. We might instinctively imagine them in their homes reading their Bibles. But people don't have personal copies of the Old Testament Scriptures at this point. So what do you imagine this "examining" looked and sounded like?

   Perhaps people gathered at the synagogue every day to listen to what Paul had to say and then opened the scrolls to the passages he worked from, reading for themselves to see if what he said lined up with what they read. Perhaps they looked up passages that they thought might conflict with his message and discussed those, or asked Paul for clarification of how his message lined up with the scrolls. Perhaps there were expressions of "Aha! I can see it!" Evidently there were others who didn't see it, who would have argued against what Paul presented. Perhaps the Jews who believed began meeting with the "Greek women of high standing as well as men" to talk about Paul's message as well. The Greek believers would have known nothing about the Old Testament, so they would have needed to be taught by the new Jewish believers.

2. What do you think it means that Paul's "spirit was provoked within him" (17:16) when he saw all the idols in Athens? Have you ever had a similar experience?

   Paul likely experienced a mixture of righteous anger and compassion. He was jealous on God's behalf for the worship being given to the idols, when such glory belongs to God alone. He was also sickened and burdened by the hold this false worship had on so many people, grieved that they were deceived and destined to perish estranged from the one true God.

3. How is Paul's presentation of the gospel in Acts 17 dramatically different from what we've heard from him before? How does this challenge or instruct us as we present the gospel to various people?

Since the people of Athens are completely unfamiliar with the Old Testament, Paul doesn't work from it as he did when he spoke to Jews in the synagogues. Instead, Paul draws from an object in their city, from the worship that was at the heart of the city and the people, and from their own literature to present the gospel. He uses the idea of a god they didn't know to present to them the one true God. He uses a truth presented by one of their poets to find common ground and then articulate the implications of that truth.

This challenges and instructs us to do our homework. If we take time to understand and consider the culture and commitments of those with whom we are sharing the gospel, we can meet them where they are, presenting the gospel in a way that connects with them and convinces them.

4. In 17:26–27 Paul says, "He made from one man every nation of mankind to live on all the face of the earth, having determined allotted periods and the boundaries of their dwelling place, that they should seek God, and perhaps feel their way toward him and find him. Yet he is actually not far from each one of us." What does this reveal about God's sovereignty over people and people groups? How can this truth help you as you think about people you know and love who are outside of Christ?

This statement portrays God actively creating from Adam all the people groups of the world, determining when and where they live, for the very purpose that they would seek him. It's a powerful picture of his sovereignty over humanity and his desire and ability to draw people to himself. When we are full of longing or fear concerning those we care about who are not in Christ, this picture can reassure us that God is at work to make himself known.

5. In 17:34 we read that those who believe include "Dionysius the Areopagite and a woman named Damaris." Why do you think Luke may have included this detail?

This shows us that Paul's preaching in Athens was not a failure. Perhaps these two names are mentioned to serve as representative figures. Dionysius's belief in Jesus shows that some who were a part of the Athenian Areopagus, which was primarily interested in defending a Greek concept of "the gods," believed in Jesus. This was huge. Damaris may have also been a distinguished Areopagite, as Epicureans and Stoics were more open to females than other cultures and groups. Luke's frequent references to women also indicate the importance and value placed on women and their witness in early Christianity. These two conversions demonstrate that the kingdom of Jesus made significant inroads into the kingdom of the world in Athens, the intellectual and philosophical center of the world in that day.

6. Paul seems to have experienced some fear about taking the gospel to the pagan Gentiles in Corinth. Does that surprise you? Disappoint you? Encourage you? Why?

It could be surprising because we've never read about Paul feeling afraid before, even though he has faced a lot of danger and rejection. Because we are often fearful about how the gospel will be received, it should encourage us to know that as experienced as Paul was, and as strong in faith as he was, Paul was also human. Like us, he felt fear in presenting the gospel to those who might reject or harm him. His obedience and his ministry fruit did not come from the fact that he was a superhuman but from his dependence on the supernatural power of the same Spirit who dwells in us.

7. When we see the evil and idolatry of our day, some of us might be tempted to ignore, withdraw, or condemn. Others might be ready to thoughtfully engage, recognizing that God has many who are his people and need to hear the word of Christ. Which of these positions comes most naturally to you? What might need to change in order for you to engage with those around you who don't know Christ and may have social, sexual, and/or political commitments that are offensive to you?

Personal response.

Let's close by asking God to give us the wisdom and courage to engage thoughtfully and helpfully with the world around us, for the cause of Christ and out of love for Christ.

Lesson 14

The Word Continued to Increase and Prevail Mightily

ACTS 18:24–20:38

Personal Bible Study

1. Read Acts 18:24–28. Luke lists several very positive things about Apollos and his teaching. And he doesn't tell us specifically what Priscilla and Aquila point out to Apollos as being not quite accurate. What do you think Luke intends for his readers to take away from these verses about Apollos's ministry?

   Apollos is a faithful brother with an effective ministry. His mistakes don't disqualify him. He needs help from others, and Priscilla and Aquila provide that help graciously, strengthening him and his ministry. This passage also shows us that it is not enough to be an eloquent or even competent teacher who is "fervent in spirit." The word of God must be handled carefully;

it's critical to get the gospel right and critical for our teaching to line up with the Scriptures, which at this point in history would have included the Old Testament and the apostolic witness (2 Pet. 3:15–16). Because the preaching of the Scriptures is what God has ordained to use to bring about salvation (Rom. 10:14), it must be presented as accurately as possible.

2. Read Acts 19:1–7. Paul explains to these men that Jesus is the person whom John the Baptist said would come after him. They have not heard of the Holy Spirit, which would mean they know nothing about what happened at Pentecost. What does this likely indicate about their spiritual condition?

   They are likely still waiting for the one whom John said would come after him, not having heard about Jesus's life and ministry, death, resurrection, and ascension. While they may be fervent disciples of John, pursuing a life of repentance and readiness for the one who would come, if they know nothing about the person and work of Jesus, they are not yet converted.

3. Read Acts 19:8–10. Paul's missionary strategy has been to set up in a major city and send coworkers into the surrounding regions. How is that working now that Paul has finally been able to come to Asia after being forbidden to do so years before (16:6)? How does that encourage you in regard to disappointments you've faced in serving Christ?

   It seems to be working effectively, since "all the residents of Asia heard the word of the Lord, both Jews and Greeks." Clearly God sent Paul to Asia at the right time. This can encourage us when we are disappointed in our service for Christ by assuring us that we can trust in God's timing and ways. A disappointment now may give way to an even better opportunity in the future.

4. Read Acts 19:11–20 with Acts 6:7 and 12:24. How is the statement in 19:20 different from the others? In what way has the word of the Lord "prevailed" in 19:11–20?

In all of the statements we read that the word of God/the word of the Lord "increased." In chapter 19, we read that it prevailed. It seems that in this story, people are not simply coming to believe but are also taking meaningful steps of repentance at great cost to themselves. Sin and evil are being pushed back in significant, tangible ways. In the situation of the Jewish exorcists wanting to appropriate the name of Jesus for their own purposes, the word of God has prevailed by enabling the evil spirit to attack the exorcists, exposing them to ridicule and causing the name of the Lord to be extolled.

5. Read Acts 19:21–27. Acts shows us how frequently false charges were brought against the apostles. But that is not the case here. What charges does Demetrius make against Paul that are true?

Paul has indeed "persuaded and turned away a great many people" from idolatry to believe that carved images are not actually gods. It's worth noting that the consequences Demetrius fears or predicts as a result of Paul's actions will also prove true: the idol-making trade and the temple of Artemis will come to nothing, and Artemis will be deposed from her magnificence as an object of worship for all Asia.

6. Read Acts 19:28–41. Earlier in this study we discussed the Pax Romana ("Roman peace"), which refers to Rome's approach to quelling riots and insurrection throughout the empire. How

does the Pax Romana work in favor of Paul and the Ephesian church in this passage?

The town clerk seems more concerned with keeping the peace than with adjudicating between Paul and the Artemis-worshiping craftsmen. Despite the fact that Demetrius seems to have a legitimate complaint, the clerk urges them to "be quiet and do nothing rash." He dismisses the assembly out of fear that they would be charged with rioting, assuring them that Artemis was not being diminished and instructing them to use the courts rather than mob violence to have their case settled.

7. Read Acts 20:1–6. Trace Paul's route as he returns to Macedonia to encourage the churches he planted there and then sails to Troas.

8. Read Acts 20:7–12. We might expect that the miracle of bringing a dead person back to life would be the most significant

thing that happens on this Lord's Day in Troas. But based on what is repeated in the passage, what does Luke seem to want us to see as most significant?

Based on the repetition and on the space given to each, Luke seems to be emphasizing the fellowship of the believers taking the Lord's Supper together and Paul's preaching of the word of God to them as a more significant aspect of his ministry than his raising Eutychus from the dead.

9. Read Acts 20:13–16, continuing to trace Paul's journey on the map.

10. Read Acts 20:17–27 and 31–35. What are some characteristics of the ministry Paul has had among the people of Ephesus?

v. 19: He served the Lord with humility and tears, enduring trials of persecution.

v. 20: In the face of opposition from the Jews, he did not shrink back from declaring anything that was profitable to their spiritual health and growth.

v. 21: He called both Jews and Greeks to repentance and faith in Jesus.

v. 25: He proclaimed the kingdom.

v. 27: He did not shrink back from declaring the whole counsel of God.

v. 31: He did not cease night or day to admonish everyone with tears.

vv. 33–34: He worked to cover his own expenses (and those of his companions) rather than seek to enrich himself by the Ephesian believers.

11. Read Acts 20:28–38. What warnings does Paul give the elders? What does he commend them to?

He warns them to be alert, to pay careful attention to themselves and to the believers of their community. He urges them to guard against false teachers who will attach themselves to the community of believers and will speak "twisted things" to draw away believers to follow after them. He commends them "to God and to the word of his grace," because the truth of the gospel has the power to build them up and provide them with the inheritance that all who are set apart to Christ can expect to receive.

Discussion Questions

1. What do you think about the idea of being shaped by words? What are some specific words that have significantly shaped you?

   Personal response.

2. What encourages or challenges you in the account of Priscilla, Aquila, and Apollos?

   Priscilla and Aquila are more concerned about the accuracy of Apollos's presentation of the gospel than they are impressed by his oratory skills and passion. Priscilla and Aquila are willing to show him his error rather than simply complain about him, and they take him aside rather than embarrass him with a public correction. Apollos is teachable, even when it means receiving instruction from a woman.

3. What do you think it means that the word of the Lord increased (Acts 6:7; 12:24)? And what do you think it means that the word of the Lord prevailed (19:20)?

   The word of God is presented as a vital force, reaching into people's lives and transforming them according to God's will. In Jesus's parable of the sower, when the seed of the gospel falls on good soil, the crop it yields is a hundred times what was sown (Luke 8:4–15). Similarly here in Acts, Luke writes of the word growing or increasing. This speaks to growth in impact, acceptance, and faithfulness to it.

By saying that the word prevailed, Luke presents the word as having power, signaling victory for the gospel of Jesus in militaristic tones. The Greek word translated as "prevail" is used earlier in the passage to say that the man with the evil spirit "overpowered" the exorcists (19:16). The word is personified as an active character in the narrative who overpowers demonic forces. In the situation of the Jewish exorcists wanting to appropriate the name of Jesus for their own purposes, the word of God prevails by enabling the evil spirit to attack the exorcists, exposing them to ridicule and causing the name of the Lord to be extolled.

4. When the new believers in Ephesus burn their magic books, which are worth a great deal of money, they demonstrate costly obedience and sanctification. We don't read that Paul admonished them to do this but that they come voluntarily, "confessing and divulging their practices" (19:18). What does this scene tell us about their repentance?

   When they see what happens with the Jewish magicians, they don't want to have anything to do with magic anymore. The Spirit uses what they witnessed to bring them to confess and renounce this lingering evil in their lives. They don't want to be tempted anymore, so they destroy what might tempt them in the future to return to that sin. They are public with their renunciation, which would make them accountable to others.

5. What kinds of costly ways might new believers today need to live out repentance and sanctification? How might those who have followed Jesus a long time still need to demonstrate costly obedience and sanctification?

New believers might find that they need to make the costly choice of renouncing a sexual relationship or activity outside of marriage, letting go of friendships that present a constant temptation to sin, or putting to death a habit that has become an addiction in their lives so that they can pursue Christ. Longtime believers may fall into some of these same sins, or they may need to make significant changes to deal with sins of apathy, hardheartedness, prayerlessness, or lack of passion for God.

6. Nancy described the word in Ephesus as a "dangerous" word. In what ways, or to what, was the word of God dangerous?

It was dangerous to idolatry and the silver shrine trade. It was dangerous to the business of those who made money from the demon-possessed girl. It was dangerous to those misusing the name of Jesus.

7. Why do you think Luke seems to want us to see the fellowship of believers around the table and the preaching of the word as more significant than the miracle of raising a person from the dead?

The apostles will not always be among God's people to work miracles, but the word will always be at work among his people, long after the apostles are gone. The Lord gave the sacrament of the Lord's Supper to strengthen his people, which it will do week after week. A miracle like the one that Eutychus experienced would be deeply encouraging to these Ephesian elders, affirming the power of God, but it would not have ongoing impact.

8. Paul said goodbye to the Ephesian elders with a clear conscience that he had declared to them "the whole counsel of

God" (20:27). Other translations speak of the whole "will" (NIV), "purpose" (NASB), or "plan" (CSB) of God. So perhaps we could say that Paul taught them everything they needed to know to live out the Christian life. If you knew you were having your last conversation with someone you love and wanted to tell them what they most need to know to live out the Christian life going forward, what kinds of things would you say?

Personal response.

Let's close by asking God to use his word to make a deep and lasting impression in our lives, shaping us into the image of Christ.

Lesson 15

Paul Resolved in His Spirit
to Go to Jerusalem

ACTS 21:1–23:35

Personal Bible Study

1. Read Acts 21:1–17, continuing to trace Paul's journey on
the map.

What message does Paul receive from other believers as he makes this journey? What is his response, and how does that influence the believers?

v. 4: *"Through the Spirit they were telling Paul not to go on to Jerusalem."*

v. 12: *"We and the people there urged him not to go up to Jerusalem."*

v. 13: *"What are you doing, weeping and breaking my heart? For I am ready not only to be imprisoned but even to die . . . for the name of the Lord Jesus."*

v. 14: *"We ceased and said, 'Let the will of the Lord be done.'"*

2. Read Romans 15:25–31; 1 Corinthians 16:1–4; and 2 Corinthians 8:1–8. What do these passages reveal about why it is important to Paul to go to Jerusalem before going to Rome?

Paul is going to Jerusalem to take financial aid from the Gentiles to the Jewish believers. He describes this gift as something the Gentiles "owe" the believers in Jerusalem, since they have "come to share in their spiritual blessings" (Rom. 15:27). It is an "act of grace" (2 Cor. 8:6, 7) by the Gentiles, a demonstration of genuine love toward their Jewish brothers and sisters, generated by the grace of Jesus at work in them. He asks the church in Rome to pray that his "service for Jerusalem may be acceptable to the saints" (Rom. 15:31). In other words, he asks them to pray that the gift he is taking to Jerusalem from the Gentiles will generate unity between the Gentiles and the Jewish believers.

3. Read Acts 21:17–26. While Paul's ministry among the Gentiles causes the elders of the church in Jerusalem to glorify God, the thousands of Jewish Christians in Jerusalem have a problem with his ministry. What have they been told about Paul?

Jewish believers in Jerusalem have been told that when Paul teaches in synagogues in Gentile territories, he tells the Jews to forsake Moses, to abandon circumcision and other Jewish customs.

What remedy do the elders suggest?

The elders recommend that Paul undertake Jewish purification rites, along with four other men, and pay the expenses of these four men who are under a vow.

4. Read Acts 21:27–36. Who stirs up the crowd and why?

Unbelieving Jews from Asia (Ephesus) see Paul in the temple and declare that he is teaching against the Jewish people, the law, and the temple. They accuse him of bringing a Gentile into the temple and thereby defiling it.

5. Read Acts 21:37–22:21. Why do you think Paul tells those seeking to kill him for being "against the people and the law" about his own history of seeking to kill Christians and seeing the risen Jesus?

Perhaps Paul wants them to see that he was once where they are. He, too, once sought to kill Jews who believed that Jesus is the Christ and that he rose from the dead. But everything changed when Paul saw and heard the risen Lord Jesus reigning in heaven. He uses the Old Testament designation for the

Messiah, "the Righteous One," to refer to Jesus, seeking to help them see the risen Jesus in that light. He explains that what he is doing and saying is a result of being commissioned by Jesus to do it—including his mission to offer salvation to the Gentiles.

6. Read Acts 22:22–29. At what point are the people no longer willing to listen to Paul? How does this reveal the most significant issue they have with Paul?

   They are no longer willing to listen when Paul says that God sent him to the Gentiles. The most offensive issue to them is that salvation could be available to outsiders instead of exclusively to them.

7. Read Acts 22:30–23:10. What does Paul say is the reason he has been put on trial? Why does this statement create violent dissension amongst his accusers?

   Paul says he is on trial "with respect to the hope and the resurrection of the dead" (23:6). This statement creates violent dissension between the Pharisee and the Sadducee members of the council because the Sadducees don't believe in a resurrection, while the Pharisees hold that it is taught by the Old Testament.

8. Read Acts 23:11. Paul has been put on trial before the council, and more trials and hardships are to come. Why would Paul have been encouraged to hear that he "must testify" about the Lord Jesus in Rome?

   This reminder of the Lord's presence with him would surely have been such a comfort to Paul. When he faces opposition from Jewish leaders, Roman rulers, a shipwreck and even a viper, he can persevere with confidence that nothing will be able to keep him from accomplishing what God has appointed him to accomplish: taking the gospel "to the end of the earth"—in other words, to Rome.

9. Read Acts 23:12–22. How do these events demonstrate that the Jews are not really interested in the law of God being kept?

   God's law clearly commands, "Do not murder." Yet these Jews have bound themselves with an oath to commit murder! They don't truly care about obedience to the Lord; they care only about suppressing and destroying Paul and his gospel message.

10. Read Acts 23:23–35. What is the "verdict" of Lysias regarding the charges the Jews have made against Paul?

    This conflict is about matters of Jewish law, not Roman law. Paul has done nothing worthy of death or imprisonment.

11. While Paul is assured that he will testify to Christ in Rome, he has to wait a long time for that to become reality. Similarly, at the heart of what it means to be a Christian is a willingness to wait for all of God's promises to become reality. What truths have you seen in Acts about God's character and how he works with his people that could help you to wait with faith for the fullness of what God has promised to his people?

    Personal response.

Discussion Questions

1. Do you agree that personal safety has become an accepted idol in our day—that it is more important to us than advancing the gospel of Jesus Christ? Why or why not?

   Personal response.

2. What message are we getting from the book of Acts about personal safety? Can you think of other places in the New Testament where Paul speaks about danger or risking life for the cause of the gospel?

In the book of Acts, we see Paul return to Lystra after having been stoned almost to the point of death (Acts 14:19), and we also see him escape from danger in a basket (Acts 9:23–25). In Acts 15:22–26, Barnabas and Paul are commended to the church in Antioch as those who have "risked their lives for the name of our Lord Jesus Christ." So Acts shows us a picture of both bold risk and wise avoidance of risk.

The whole of the New Testament presents faithful discipleship as reckoning with the reality of persecution and suffering for the cause of Christ. In 2 Corinthians 11:23–27, Paul points to the danger he has faced from numerous threats for the cause of the gospel as a demonstration of his credibility as an apostle. In 1 Corinthians 15:30, when he is arguing for the significance of the resurrection, Paul asks the rhetorical question, "Why are we in danger every hour?" In other words, the reality of resurrection is what makes facing danger worth it to Paul.

Clearly we need God-given wisdom to know when to risk boldly and when to avoid risk. The Bible specifically tells us to ask God for wisdom and promises that he will give it (James 1:5). We can't presume that walking in the wisdom he imparts to us will necessarily mean that we will be spared from harm. We see in the Scriptures, as well as throughout history, that God's wise plan has often included the suffer-

ing of those who belong to him. But we can expect that the wisdom he gives us will strengthen us to face whatever he ordains for us with faith.

3. Paul knows that he will face suffering in Jerusalem. Why is he so determined to go there anyway? What does he hope this trip will accomplish?

Paul wants to take the financial gift from the Gentiles to the Jews facing famine in Jerusalem. He wants to help the believers in Jerusalem through this gift. But his deeper motivation is to connect and unify the Gentile and Jewish believers in mutual service and affection. Paul was appointed by God to be the apostle to the Gentiles, but he knows that there is not to be a separate Gentile church. As a Jew sent to the Gentiles, Paul sees it as part of his mission to connect Jewish and Gentile believers for the flourishing of the church.

4. Why do you think Paul is willing to submit to an Old Testament purification ritual and to pay the cost for four men under a Nazirite vow?

Paul lives as a Jew among Jews, embracing Jewish ceremony and customs, even though he knows that those things are not required for salvation and that Jesus has fulfilled it all. He does not carry out these customs in order to secure his salvation, or as a matter of necessary obedience, but as a matter of freedom.

The Nazirite vow described in Numbers 6 was taken by those who desired to yield themselves to God completely. "The Nazirite vow, which appears in Numbers 6:1-21, has five features. It is voluntary, can be done by either men or women, has a specific time frame, has specific requirements and restrictions, and at its conclusion a sacrifice is offered."[1]

Paul must have recognized that there was spiritual value in going through the act of making and carrying out such a vow to God, even though it was not required under the new covenant.

Paul is willing to pay the cost for the four men to complete their vow because he recognizes it would have spiritual value to those making the vow. He also hopes it will confirm to Jewish believers in Jerusalem that he is not against engaging in Jewish customs as long as they are not required for salvation.

In the Old Testament, men engaged in holy war sometimes took a Nazirite vow. (A literal translation of the opening of Deborah's song in Judges 5:2 says, "Because of the flowing hair of the fighters in Israel, because the people gave themselves freely, give praise to the Lord.") At the end of the military campaign, they shaved off their hair and dedicated it to God on the altar. Paul saw his missionary journeys as holy war campaigns, taking new territory for the gospel similar to the way Joshua took possession of the promised land. But Paul waged war with the sword of the Spirit as he preached the gospel of Christ. Instead of slaying his enemies, he pled and worked for their salvation.

If we understand that Paul saw himself as engaged in holy war, it makes sense that he entered into a Nazirite vow as a symbol of his desire to yield himself to God completely for the purposes of building Christ's kingdom. We're told in Acts 18 that Paul remained at Corinth for eighteen months, and then, coming

---

1   "What is the Nazirite/Nazarite vow?" Got Questions, accessed July 20, 2023, https://www.gotquestions.org/.

to the end of his second missionary journey he "cut his hair, for he was under a vow" (18:18). Perhaps Paul saw himself as having completed a new phase of holy war against the powers of darkness, taking new territory for the kingdom of Jesus, and the cutting of his hair indicated he had completed his vow.

5. After Paul was nearly torn to pieces by the Jewish mob, "the Lord stood by him" and assured him that he would "testify also in Rome" (23:11). How would that have made a difference to Paul over the coming years he spent in custody?

Surely Paul was deeply encouraged to know that he was not alone. What a comfort to be reassured that Jesus himself stood by him as he faced such significant suffering for declaring his hope in Jesus! Sometimes we can assume that we must be doing something wrong if we suffer this much. But the presence of Jesus with Paul assured him that he had the approval of Jesus. Jesus's instruction to Paul to "take courage" and his affirmation that Paul would testify to him in Rome must have helped Paul to persevere in faith that nothing could stop him from fulfilling the plans and purposes God had for him. He would succeed in taking the gospel "to the end of the earth" (Acts 1:8).

6. Has there been a low time in your life when you sensed "the Lord stood by" you? How have you experienced Jesus's comfort and presence in the midst of suffering?

Personal response.

7. Nancy said, "We have an incredible impulse toward self-preservation and very little inclination toward self-denial. It makes us wonder if it is really possible that we could deny

ourselves, take up our cross, and follow Jesus." What do you think it takes for people like you and me to overcome self-preservation and to embrace self-denial and even danger? How could we help each other do this more?

Personal response.

Let's close by asking God to give us the grace and wisdom to embrace self-denial and take appropriate risks for the sake of the gospel.

Lesson 16

I Always Take Pains to Have a Clear Conscience toward God and Man

ACTS 24:1–26:32

Personal Bible Study

1. Read Acts 24:1–21. From these verses, what are the three "crimes" Paul is charged with? How does he respond to each of those charges?

Charge against Paul	Paul's response to the charge
v. 5a: *Stirs up riots among Jews throughout the world.*	vv. 10–13: *I went to the temple to worship and did not dispute with anyone or stir up a crowd in the temple or in synagogues.*
v. 5b: *Is a ringleader of the sect of the Nazarenes.*	vv. 14–16: *I worship the same God they do, believe everything in the same Scriptures, and share the same hope in a resurrection. Because I believe in a judgment to come at the resurrection, I keep a clear conscience before God and man.*
v. 6: *Tried to profane the temple.*	vv. 17–19: *I came to bring alms to the Jewish people and to present offerings at the temple, not to profane the temple. The people who accused me of profaning the temple should be here to present their evidence.*

2. Read Acts 24:22–27. Paul reasons with Felix about righteousness, self-control, and the coming judgment. Why do you think each of these things might have caused Felix to respond with alarm? (A few notes that might be helpful: Paul would have written his letter to the Romans by this point, so you might consider his teaching on righteousness in Rom. 3:10–12, 21–26. Felix was known to be a cruel tyrant. According to Josephus, Felix seduced and lured Drusilla away from her first husband to make her his third wife.)

Righteousness: *Paul taught clearly that no one is righteous and that perfect righteousness is required to stand before a holy God. Felix would have been alarmed at his own inability to meet that standard. This is an offensive message to anyone who wants to believe he is generally a pretty good person and tries to do the right thing, who doesn't want to be dependent on anyone or anything.*

Self-control: *Since Felix and Drusilla's marriage was founded on lust and a lack of self-control, Felix would have been alarmed by his obvious inability to control himself, marking him out as one who does not belong to God.*

The coming judgment: *No one wants to hear that punishment is coming for him. If Felix felt some level of conviction or condemnation after Paul's reasoning with him about righteousness and self-control (and his lack thereof), he would have felt alarmed to think about the prospect of judgment.*

3. Read Acts 25:1–12. While the charges made against Paul before Festus are not articulated here, we can make an assump-

tion about the charges based on Paul's defense in verse 8. What new accusation has been added to the charges made against him in the earlier trial before Felix?

Previously the charges were focused on Paul's alleged offenses against the Jews and the temple; now he is apparently being accused of crimes "against Caesar."

4. Read Acts 25:13–27. What does Festus make of the charges against Paul? What problem does this create for Festus?

Festus sees the charges as "points of dispute . . . about their own religion," not as true evils (vv. 18–19). He finds that Paul has "done nothing deserving death" (v. 25). Paul has appealed to go to Rome, his right as a Roman citizen. But Festus can't identify any charges that he can write in a letter to Caesar that are worthy of Caesar's consideration.

5. Read Acts 26:1–11. What does Paul share with the Pharisees who are among his accusers? (See also Acts 23:6 and 24:15.)

He has lived by their strict rules since his youth, and he shares their hope in God's promise of the resurrection of the dead. He used to share their opposition to Jesus of Nazareth and their persecution of his followers in raging fury—the same fury the Pharisees now have against Paul.

6. Read Acts 26:12–15. What evidence for the resurrection of Jesus does Paul offer in these verses?

Paul describes his own experience of seeing the radiant, risen Jesus shining from heaven and hearing his voice identify himself as Jesus.

7. Read Acts 26:16–23. How does Paul articulate what it means
    to be saved in the following verses?

    vv. 17–18: *To be saved is to have your eyes opened to see who Jesus
    is, to turn from darkness to light and from the power of Satan to
    the power of God. It is to receive forgiveness of sins and a place
    in God's family. It is to be set apart as belonging to God by faith.*

    v. 20: *To be saved is to have repented and turned to God in such
    a way that you live a new life in keeping with that repentance.*

8. Read Acts 26:24–32. How is Paul's interaction with Agrippa
    consistent with the whole of his ministry up to this point?

    *Paul boldly proclaims the gospel of Jesus Christ and calls all
    people to follow him. He doesn't shrink back from declaring the
    good news of the kingdom and calling people to repent, even
    in court proceedings before a king!*

9. By the time Paul stands in these various courts, he has already
    written to the believers in Rome, "Let every person be subject
    to the governing authorities" (Rom. 13:1). How do you see
    Paul living out his own instructions? How does his example
    challenge you as you evaluate your attitudes and actions toward
    governing authorities?

    Personal response.

Discussion Questions

1. Is it really possible to be self-aware about our pervasive sinful-
    ness, especially at the level of inner thoughts and motives, and
    yet have a clear conscience? Why or why not?

We know that sanctification is a lifelong process and that we will never attain sinless perfection in this life, but we can seek to keep short accounts with God. As we ask him to reveal our sin to us (Ps. 139:23–24), confess it to him (1 John 1:9), and perhaps confess to other trusted believers (James 5:6), we can expect to receive his forgiveness and cleansing and thereby have a clear conscience.

Believers who are particularly aware of their own remaining sin at the heart level may find it difficult to rest in the cleansing work of Christ, instead plagued by an overactive conscience. But John tells those whose hearts condemn them in this way that "God is greater than our heart, and he knows everything" (1 John 3:20–24). And the writer of Hebrews reassures us that because we have Jesus as our great high priest, we can and should "draw near with a true heart in full assurance of faith, with our hearts sprinkled clean from an evil conscience" (Heb. 10:21–22).

2. What are some ways we try to deal with a sullied conscience? What is the good news of the gospel for those of us with a sullied conscience?

Some people seek to silence their conscience through distraction, rebellion, addiction, or denial. And it's sobering to realize that the more we do this, the more our conscience becomes seared. Those who habitually silence the Spirit's voice of conviction should tremble to realize they are headed in the direction of no longer hearing his voice at all (Heb. 3:15).

But the good news of the gospel is that only one person has ever had a perfectly clear conscience, and his blood is enough to pay the price for all of the sin that has polluted or seared our consciences (Heb. 9:14). His love for us, demonstrated at the cross, assures us that "if we confess our sins, he is faithful and just to forgive us our sins and to cleanse us from all unrighteousness" (1 John 1:9).

3. Throughout Acts, and again here, the message of the apostles has been summarized as the resurrection from or of the dead (4:2; 17:32; 23:6; 24:21). Hopefully we've gotten clear on the meaning of this phrase, but just in case, what do the apostles mean when they say that their message or hope is the resurrection of the dead?

   When the apostles speak about the resurrection of the dead, the phrase encompasses a host of realities wrapped up with the coming of the Messiah. These include the resurrection of Jesus as the firstfruits of all who will rise from the dead; the bodily resurrection of the just and the unjust (Rom. 14:10); the glorification of the saints; the destruction of the devil and the end of evil; the establishment of the new creation; and final judgment.

4. In 24:25 we're told that Paul reasons with Felix about righteousness, self-control, and the coming judgment. Why do you think each of these things might have caused Felix to respond with alarm? (A few notes that might be helpful: Paul would have written his letter to the Romans by this point, so you might consider his teaching on righteousness in Rom. 3:10–12, 21–26. Felix was known to be a cruel tyrant. According to Josephus, Felix seduced and lured Drusilla away from her first husband to make her his third wife.)

Righteousness: *Paul taught that no one is righteous and that perfect righteousness is required to stand before a holy God. Felix would have been alarmed at his own inability to meet that standard. This is an offensive message to anyone who wants to believe he is generally a pretty good person and tries to do the right thing, who doesn't want to be dependent on anyone or anything.*

Self-control: *Since Felix and Drusilla's marriage was founded on lust and a lack of self-control, Felix would have been alarmed by his obvious inability to control himself, marking him out as one who does not belong to God.*

The coming judgment: *No one wants to hear that punishment is coming for him. If Felix felt some level of conviction or condemnation after Paul's reasoning with him about righteousness and self-control (and his lack thereof), he would have felt alarmed to think about the prospect of judgment.*

5. Read Romans 12:14–13:7, which Paul has already written by the time he stands before Felix, Festus, and Agrippa. How do you see Paul living out his own instructions? How does his example challenge you as you evaluate your attitudes and actions toward governing authorities?

Paul speaks the truth and offers the blessing of salvation to those who persecute him, while also reminding them of God's certain judgment against those who reject his Son. Paul has sought to live peaceably with all, going to great lengths to defuse tensions and demonstrate to the Jews that he is not against them or their customs. Paul never demonstrates any desire for vengeance. He is not overcome by the evil inflicted on him but overcomes that evil with good. Paul interacts respectfully with all the governing authorities over him, even though they are often harsh, corrupt, unjust, and incompetent. He can say he has a good conscience before God and man because he has operated in subjection to their authority.

6. In her introduction, Nancy asked, "What does it really mean to be saved?" In Acts 26:16–23, Paul articulates what it means to be saved. As we approach the end of this study, how has your understanding of salvation changed or developed? What have you grown to appreciate about God's outworking of his salvation plan?

   Personal response.

Let's close by thanking God for making it possible to live with a clear conscience because of the sacrifice of Jesus and for our increasing grasp of what it means that we have been saved, are being saved, and will be saved.

Lesson 17

It Will Be Exactly as I Have Been Told

ACTS 27:1–28:31

Personal Bible Study

1. Read Acts 27:1–28:1. Draw arrows on the map below to trace the journey of the ship carrying Paul; his companions, Aristarchus and Luke; his Roman Centurion guard, Julius; and another 272 people from Caesarea to Malta.

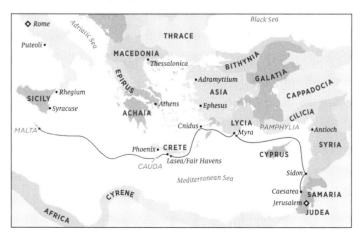

2. While Paul does not receive a miraculous deliverance from the stormy seas or ship that is breaking apart, he does receive supernatural revelation that gives him confidence. What is it?

    An angel of God tells him, "Do not be afraid, Paul; you must stand before Caesar. And behold, God has granted you all those who sail with you" (27:24). Paul knows that he and everyone else on the ship will survive whatever comes because God is sovereignly overseeing the trip and Paul's appearance before Caesar in Rome.

    How does he respond to this revelation?

    Paul believes that what God has told him through his angel is exactly what will take place. He encourages the other people on the ship to take heart (though not before getting in an "I told you so" in verse 21!).

    How does this revelation relate to an earlier message from Jesus in Acts 23:11?

    This confirms and repeats the Lord's message to Paul in 23:11, where he was told to take courage because he "must testify also in Rome."

3. In Acts 27:20, Luke writes that "all hope of our being saved was at last abandoned." But Paul is "saved" from many things in chapter 27. What are they?

    v. 24: He is saved from fear when God speaks to him in a vision.

    vv. 30–32: His life is saved when the soldiers prevent the sailors from escaping.

    vv. 33–36: He is saved from starvation.

vv. 42–43: *His life is saved when the centurion prevents the soldiers from killing him along with the other prisoners.*

v. 44: *He is saved from drowning after the ship falls apart.*

4. Read Acts 28:1–10. In what ways are these events also about the power of God to save?

Paul is miraculously saved from the poison of the viper (v. 3). Publius's father is healed (v. 8), and others with diseases are cured (v. 9). Paul and his companions are "saved" through the kindness of the Maltese, who welcome them (v. 2) and provide for their needs so that they can survive the rest of their journey (v. 10).

5. Though we're not told explicitly what happens on Malta, we could probably rightly assume a couple of things. Based on the events of Acts 14:8–15, how do you think Paul responds when the Maltese think he is a god?

In Lystra, Paul and Barnabas tore their clothes at the very idea that the people could think they were gods. They used the opportunity to tell them about the true and living God, the maker of heaven and earth. So it is likely that Paul quickly sets the Maltese straight and preaches the gospel to them.

Based on what Paul has done everywhere he has gone, and specifically during his two years in Ephesus (Acts 19:10–11), what could we assume is happening during Paul's three months on Malta in addition to physical healing?

Over the two years Paul was in Ephesus, while he was performing miracles, "all the residents of Asia heard the word of the Lord."

Everywhere he brought physical healing, he also spoke the word of God to people and called them to repentance and belief. So we could assume that the same is happening here—as Paul heals people physically, he offers them salvation in Jesus Christ.

6. Read Acts 28:11–23, continuing to trace Paul's route on the map found in question 1.

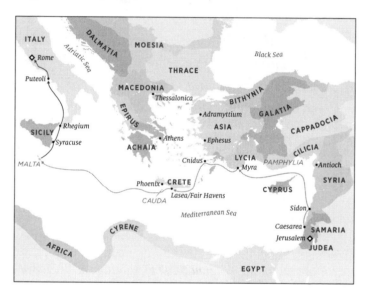

In what way is Paul's pattern of ministry in Rome the same as it has been everywhere else?

Paul goes first to the Jews, testifying to the kingdom of God and trying to convince them from the law of Moses and the prophets that Jesus is the Christ.

7. Read Acts 28:24–28. Put into your own words what Paul communicates to the unbelieving Jews in Rome by quoting Isaiah 6:9–10 to them.

Paul is saying, "You are like your Israelite ancestors who heard God's word, but their hearts were too dull to listen, understand, and respond in repentance and faith. The salvation of God has come to the Gentiles, just as the Old Testament said it would. They will listen. God's purposes for the salvation of a people for himself from every nation of the earth cannot be thwarted by your resistance and rejection."

8. While Luke is an excellent and careful historian, he is not simply writing to inform. He is writing to persuade. What do you think he wants his first reader, Theophilus, and his additional readers (including us) to believe and do based on the story he has told us in Acts? List at least four or five things.

- *The resurrection of Jesus and the sending of the Holy Spirit inaugurates the fulfillment of all the Old Testament promises.*
- *The gospel spreads through the preaching of the word of Christ.*
- *God has always planned for his salvation to spread to all nations.*
- *The gospel is unstoppable. It spreads not in spite of suffering and opposition, but through opposition and suffering.*
- *The resurrection of Jesus assures us of a greater resurrection to come.*
- *God works in and through the local church.*

9. Throughout this study, we've seen the Holy Spirit at work in and through his people in many ways. How have you gained a greater appreciation for what it means to have the Spirit's

power at work in and through your life? How could you cultivate more of an awareness or appreciation of the Spirit's work in your life?

Many of us tend to think about the Spirit's work in terms of individual personal growth, such as the ways we display the fruit of the Spirit. And that is significant. But throughout Acts, we see an emphasis on the Spirit's work in and through his church—the spread of the gospel and the strengthening of churches. This might challenge us to ask ourselves: How much is my life built around that priority? Do I want the Spirit's power to work in me simply so that I can be more patient or peaceful, or do I also long for his power to work in me so that more people will come to know him and so that his church can be built up?

We might cultivate awareness of the Spirit's work by paying more attention to and praying about what Scripture teaches regarding his purposes: Welcome his conviction. Receive his comfort rather than seeking comfort elsewhere. Credit ministry successes to his power, not merely human wisdom or talent. Recognize that in every problem, the ultimate solution is not human ingenuity or effort but the Spirit's power to change human hearts and produce fruit. Ask him to make his fruit more evident in our lives and in the lives of our brothers and sisters.

Discussion Questions

1. We could title Acts 27–28 "God's Power to Save." How do we see God's power to save in these chapters?

- *Paul is saved from fear when God speaks to him in a vision (27:24).*
- *Soldiers are saved when they prevent the sailors from escaping (27:30–32).*
- *Ship passengers are saved from starvation/hunger (27:33–36).*
- *Paul and the other prisoners are saved from the soldiers who plan to kill them (27:42–43).*
- *All are saved from drowning after the ship falls apart in the storm (27:44).*
- *Paul is miraculously saved from the poison of the viper (28:3).*
- *The father of the chief man of the island is healed, and many others with diseases are cured (28:8–9).*
- *Paul and his companions are saved through the kindness of the Maltese, who welcome them (28:2) and provide for their needs so that they can survive the rest of their journey (28:10).*

2. In what ways is Paul's whole life a testimony to God's power to save?

   Paul was saved from unbelief and pride. He was saved from a life of hating the gospel to a life of embracing and declaring the gospel. He was saved from pharisaical religiosity to a grace-filled life of genuine faith.

3. Paul has faith in God that the safe passage of all on the ship to Rome will be exactly as he has been told. What are some promises in the Bible that you can take hold of, having full confidence that it will be exactly as you have been told?

"And behold, I am with you always, to the end of the age" (Matt. 28:20).

"I have said these things to you, that in me you may have peace. In the world you will have tribulation. But take heart; I have overcome the world" (John 16:33).

"If God is for us, who can be against us? He who did not spare his own Son but gave him up for us all, how will he not also with him graciously give us all things?" (Rom. 8:31–32).

"For I am sure that neither death nor life, nor angels nor rulers, nor things present nor things to come, nor powers, nor height nor depth, nor anything else in all creation, will be able to separate us from the love of God in Christ Jesus our Lord" (Rom. 8:38–39).

"The Lord is at hand; do not be anxious about anything, but in everything by prayer and supplication with thanksgiving let your requests be made known to God. And the peace of God, which surpasses all understanding, will guard your hearts and your minds in Christ Jesus" (Phil. 4:5b–7).

"For because he himself has suffered when tempted, he is able to help those who are being tempted" (Heb. 2:18).

"Let us then with confidence draw near to the throne of grace, that we may receive mercy and find grace to help in time of need" (Heb. 4:16).

"For the moment all discipline seems painful rather than pleasant, but later it yields the peaceful fruit of righteousness to those who have been trained by it" (Heb. 12:11).

"If any of you lacks wisdom, let him ask God, who gives generously to all without reproach, and it will be given him" (James 1:5).

"God opposes to the proud but gives grace to the humble" (1 Pet. 5:5).

"His divine power has granted to us all things that pertain to life and godliness, through the knowledge of him who called us to his own glory and excellence, by which he has granted to us his precious and very great promises, so that through them you may become partakers of the divine nature, having escaped from the corruption that is in the world because of sinful desire" (2 Pet. 1:3–4).

4. What are some Bible verses that people take hold of as "promises," but that aren't really promises we can claim? What is the danger of clinging to these verses as promises?

   "Train up a child in the way he should go; even when he is old he will not depart from it" (Prov. 22:6). This (as well as most, if not all, other proverbs) is a principle, not a promise. It describes how life usually works in the world. It does not provide a guarantee but rather a statement of something that generally proves true.

   "For I know the plans I have for you, declares the LORD, plans for welfare and not for evil, to give you a future and a hope" (Jer. 29:11). This is a promise made to a specific group of people (the exiles from Judah) at a particular time (during their exile in Babylon), referring to a specific future (their return to the land). The reason they needed to be told that God had plans

for their welfare was that everything about their circumstances suggested the opposite. Yes, God does have a future and a hope for us, but that promise comes to us in places like Revelation 21:1–6! We need to consider that the exiles lived seventy years—a lifetime—not getting what they hoped for. The same may be true for us.

These examples reflect the importance of paying attention to context as we study Scripture and look for God's promises to us. Rather than yank encouraging verses out of context, we must take care to consider the original audience and the type of literature. Proverbs aren't meant to be promises. Narratives are often descriptive and/or rooted in a particular character and time rather than prescriptive or meant for universal application. Prophecies must be first considered in light of the original author's intended meaning. Ignoring these principles of Bible study (or of reading comprehension more broadly) can lead us to feel disillusioned or disappointed with God when the "promises" we thought he made don't turn out to be reliable.

5. Throughout the book of Acts, opposition to the gospel has come from many sources, both human and supernatural. List as many sources as you can remember: Who has been against the gospel? What has this book shown us about opposition to the gospel?

Opposition comes from the religious leaders in Jerusalem, unbelieving Jews in Jerusalem and throughout the Gentile world, demonic spirits, governmental authorities, false believers, and businesspeople who find their idol business threatened. The book of Acts has shown us God's sovereignty over all opposition to the gospel. Its spread cannot be thwarted; rather, the Lord uses even opposition to accomplish his purposes.

6. Do you think Acts ends on a victorious note? Why or why not?

Acts may seem to end on a note of defeat, as Paul is still under house arrest in Rome. We don't know exactly when and how Paul died, but it is entirely possible that Paul found himself in Rome in the midst of Nero's persecution following the great fire and was put to death there. But the final verse of Acts speaks of Paul accomplishing what God appointed him to do—preaching the gospel to Gentiles at the end of the earth, in Rome. He is doing so "with all boldness and without hindrance," which indicates victory over his circumstances and opposition.

7. Back in the introduction, we looked at several possible titles for this book. Having now worked your way through Acts, in what way do you see each of these as a possibility?

- The Acts of the Apostles
- The Acts of the Holy Spirit
- The Acts of the Preached Word
- The Acts of the Enthroned Lord Jesus

The apostles are the primary human actors, the vessels through which God carries out his plan. The Holy Spirit is the power at work in every human action, from proclaiming the gospel to performing signs and wonders to repenting and believing in Jesus. The preached word is the means the apostles use to draw people to God—throughout Acts, we see the word spreading, increasing, and multiplying. And through the apostles, the Spirit, and the word, the enthroned Lord Jesus himself is at work. He is still active from heaven, providing for his disciples and adding believers to his church.

8. When Luke began writing the first of his two-book series, the Gospel of Luke, he wrote, "It seemed good to me also, having followed all things closely for some time past, to write an orderly account for you, most excellent Theophilus, that you may have certainty concerning the things you have been taught" (Luke 1:3–4). What can you take away with certainty from the things you have seen in Acts?

- *The salvation of God through Jesus Christ is for all people.*
- *God has always intended to gather a people for himself from every nation.*
- *The gospel divides. Some believe and are saved; others reject and are condemned.*
- *The spread of the gospel message is unstoppable. It cannot be thwarted by any opposition.*
- *The gospel spreads in the world, not in spite of the suffering and persecution of believers but often specifically through the suffering of believers.*
- *Christianity (called "the Way" in Acts) is not a new religion. Rather, it is the embrace of the fulfillment of promises made to Israel. It is the climax of God's original plan of salvation. Luke stresses the continuity between the old and the new in God's plan of salvation.*

- *Just as the death of Jesus was not a failure of God's plan, but the fulfillment of his plan, so the rejection of the gospel by the Jews was not a failure of God's plan, but the fulfillment of his plan to make salvation available to the Gentiles.*
- *The resurrection of Jesus as the firstborn from the dead assures us of a greater resurrection to come.*
- *Jesus pours out his Spirit on all who put their faith in him.*
- *The Holy Spirit is at work through his people by his word to call all who will repent and believe into the kingdom of Jesus Christ.*

9. How will your certainty about these truths impact the way you live?

   Personal response.

Let's close by asking the Spirit who came at Pentecost to indwell his people, and who dwells in us even now, to implant these truths from Acts deep in our souls. Let's ask him to increase our confidence in God's salvation and expand our love for people, from those around us to those who are at the ends of the earth.

GROUP DISCUSSION
QUESTIONS

for Copying and Distributing to Participants

Introduction: Acts of the Apostles

Discussion Questions

1. Some of us may have studied Acts before, while others of us may be completely new to it. When you think about the book of Acts (the largest book of the New Testament), what do you already know—or think you know—about it?

2. As we trace the progress of the gospel in Acts, it will be helpful for us to consult various maps of the known world in the first century. Take a moment to explore your Bible. What map(s) do you find that might prove helpful during this study?

3. Nancy talked about the personal Bible study questions she has prepared to help us to get into the text of Acts. Are you planning to work through the personal Bible study prior to each session? Where can you make time in your schedule for completing it?

4. Nancy presented various possible titles for the book of Acts: Acts of the Apostles, Acts of the Holy Spirit, Acts of the Preached Word, and Acts of the Enthroned Lord Jesus. How are each of these "actors" significant in accomplishing the salvation of God?

5. The central aim of Acts is to assure us that the Lord Jesus is at work by his Spirit, through the word of God preached and written by the apostles, to save a vast people for himself. Why

might Luke's original audience have needed that assurance? Why might we need that assurance today?

6. Salvation is past, present, and future, so we can rightly say, "I have been saved; I am being saved; I will be saved." How does this challenge your thinking about what it means to be "saved"? What are we being saved from in each of these three aspects of salvation?

7. What do you personally hope to get out of this study of Acts?

Let's close by praying that God will impress upon us the wonders of his salvation plan for his people as we work our way through this study of Acts.

Lesson 1

Discussion Questions

You Will Be My Witnesses

ACTS 1:1–26

1. Luke begins by referring to his Gospel, which was about what Jesus "began to do and teach" (Acts 1:1). This implies that Acts is about what Jesus continued to do and teach after his ascension. Why is it important for us to recognize that Jesus continues to "do and teach" from his throne in heaven?

2. Why is the ascension of Jesus significant? Why do you think we give so much less attention to it than to his incarnation, death, and resurrection?

3. What kinds of things do you think Jesus discussed with the apostles when he spent forty days with them "speaking about the kingdom of God" (Acts 1:3)?

4. How would the Old Testament prophets have shaped how the apostles thought about the restoration of Israel?

5. If you were an ordinary Israelite in the Old Testament era, why might you have longed for the day when "the promise of the Father," the indwelling of the Holy Spirit in all believers, would become a reality?

6. Jesus tells the apostles that they would receive power to be his witnesses "in Jerusalem and in all Judea and Samaria, and to the end of the earth" (Acts 1:8). In what ways would they need divine power to accomplish this task?

7. Can the statement "You will be my witnesses" be applied directly to us today? Why or why not?

8. Nancy suggests that instead of thinking of ourselves as "witnesses," we should think of ourselves as "proclaimers." What is the difference? How might this distinction impact how we approach our mission?

9. Though we are proclaimers rather than witnesses, we need the same divine power these eyewitnesses needed to accomplish their task. And that power is available to us! In what ways do we need the Holy Spirit's power to accomplish our task?

Let's close by praying for each other to receive divine power for the task of proclaiming what the apostles have handed down to us.

Lesson 2

Discussion Questions

I Will Pour Out My Spirit

ACTS 2:1–47

1. The personal Bible study took you to some Old Testament examples where wind and fire were evidence of earthly and heavenly realms coming together. And perhaps you can think of some others. What kinds of things do the fire and wind accomplish or represent?

2. We're told that the 120 new believers in Christ are able to speak in the languages of the devout Jews and proselytes gathered in Jerusalem, telling them about "the mighty works of God" (2:11). What kinds of things do you think they might have said?

3. Peter explains Pentecost as a fulfillment of Joel's prophecy that the Spirit would be poured out on all people so that they could understand and articulate the message of salvation in Christ. How was this experience of the Spirit different from what ordinary believers experienced throughout the Old Testament?

4. At the end of his sermon (2:36), Peter says that based on what he has presented, they should "know for certain that God has made [Jesus] both Lord and Christ." What do you think it

would have been like to be in that crowd on that day? What kinds of things might those in the crowd have been thinking?

5. Imagine being part of a new church with three thousand new believers who have come out of being devout followers of Judaism and speak many different languages. What challenges would such a church face?

6. How do we see the Spirit at work empowering this new community in Acts 2:42–47? What aspects of their life together do you find especially appealing?

7. One way to think through the impact of Pentecost is to consider what would be different if it had not happened. How would your life be different if Jesus had ascended and begun to reign but had not given the Holy Spirit to dwell in you?

Let's pray, thanking God for the Holy Spirit and asking him to purify us with his fire, to breathe his life into us by his Spirit. Let's ask him to help us welcome the work of the Holy Spirit in our lives, even though it may push us beyond our comfort zones.

Lesson 3

Discussion Questions

In Jesus the Resurrection from the Dead

ACTS 3:1–4:31

1. In the personal Bible study, you were asked to read passages from Isaiah, Jeremiah, Zephaniah, and Micah. What commonalities did you see? How do you think these passages relate to "in Jesus the resurrection of the dead" (Acts 4:2)?

2. How is Peter's message in Acts 3:11–21 an example to follow in presenting the gospel?

3. Take turns putting 3:19–21 in your own words. How would you share the substance of Peter's gospel presentation with those around you today?

4. What in Peter and John's message annoyed the priests, the captain of the temple, and the Sadducees?

5. What do you think Peter is trying to communicate by quoting Psalm 2 in his prayer in Acts 4:25–28? (Consider reading the whole psalm together.) What is he saying about Jesus, and about the religious leaders who had told them not to speak? How do you think it would have helped these first believers to see their experience in light of Psalm 2?

6. When you consider the background of the disciples and the way they abandoned Jesus at his arrest and crucifixion, how do you explain the boldness of Peter and John in these chapters?

7. What do you think are the greatest hindrances to our ability or willingness to "speak the word of God with boldness"? What do you think could happen if you were bolder?

Let's pray, asking for boldness to speak the word of God in specific situations or settings in our lives.

Lesson 4

Discussion Questions

You Will Not Be Able to Overthrow Them

ACTS 4:32–5:42

1. In Acts 4:32 we read that this new community was "of one heart and soul." What would it be like to be part of a community like this? What hinders this kind of unity in the church, both then and now?

2. How have you witnessed generosity among brothers and sisters in Christ? What are some ways you'd like to see more generosity in the church?

3. When you read the story of Ananias and Sapphira, how do you find yourself responding emotionally? Are you horrified, offended, relieved, satisfied? Why?

4. What are some things we might do or say to appear more spiritual than we really are? What motivates this kind of pretending?

5. In Acts 5:17 we read that the high priest and the party of the Sadducees were filled with jealousy because people were bringing their sick to the apostles and they were being healed. Jealousy is a terrible thing. Even worse is jealousy over the impact of someone else's genuine ministry impact. Have you

ever felt this kind of jealousy or had it directed toward you? What can we do to fight envy when we see God using someone else in a way we wish he was using us?

6. The story of the new-covenant community has hardly gotten started when we read about this event with Ananias and Sapphira. And it is so much different than what we've read so far. What do you think Luke wants his readers to take away from it?

7. The religious council in Jerusalem seeks to silence the apostles through intimidation, imprisonment, and beatings. While many believers around the world face that exact treatment today, others face more subtle tactics. What are some other ways people seek to intimidate Christians and prevent them from speaking about Christ today?

8. How do you explain the apostles' response to being beaten in Acts 5:41–42?

9. While we may believe in theory that the gospel is unstoppable, sometimes it can be hard to believe this when we face opposition, or when we consider the opposition to the gospel around the world. What difference do you think it could make in your life, or in ministries that you are a part of, to really believe that the gospel is unstoppable?

Let's close by asking the Lord to show us any spiritual hypocrisy or ministry envy that needs to be confessed and forsaken. Let's ask him to fill us with courage to speak of him and supernatural joy when we suffer for doing so.

Lesson 5

Discussion Questions

The Most High Does Not Dwell
in Houses Made by Hands

ACTS 6:1–7:60

1. How does Acts 6:7 provide a sort of "progress report" on the outworking of Acts 1:8? How do you think the temple leaders feel about these developments?

2. In many ways, the interaction between Stephen and his accusers is hard to follow. Just to make sure we're all clear, what are the two charges made against Stephen? And how would you summarize his response to those charges?

3. Think back through Stephen's argument (without looking, if you can!) and trace the location of God's presence or glory throughout Israel's history.

4. What do we learn about God as we trace where his presence moved throughout the history of his people? (For a clear statement of God's intention, see Ex. 29:45–46.)

5. Where is God's presence or glory found today? How does this reality challenge or encourage you?

6. Why is it likely not surprising to Stephen that they want to kill him?

7. What might have comforted Stephen as he faced death?

8. How can Stephen's death provide comfort to us as believers in life and in death?

Let's close by praying for our brothers and sisters around the world who face the kind of treatment Stephen suffered—that they would have courage to stand firm in their faith and joy as they anticipate seeing his glory.

Lesson 6

Discussion Questions

They Were All Scattered

ACTS 8:1–40

1. Read Ezekiel 37:15–19 together. How is this becoming reality in Acts 8?

2. Imagine that you are a Samaritan living in Samaria when Philip comes to town. What kinds of things are you hearing and witnessing? By the time Philip, Peter, and John leave, how has your life changed?

3. In what ways is Jesus a gatherer? Consider his earthly ministry, death, resurrection, ascension, sending his Spirit, present reign, and promised return.

4. Nancy confessed that she has a long way to go to be a gatherer like Jesus is a gatherer. Can you relate to that? What steps could you take to become more of a gatherer like Jesus?

5. In what ways is Simon the magician similar to Achan (Josh. 7:10–21), Judas (Matt. 26:14–16), and Ananias and Sapphira (Acts 5:1–11)? What does this indicate about him?

6. Nancy challenged us to examine ourselves rather than focus on Simon the magician. What are some ways people might

be tempted to use Jesus for their own ends rather than loving and serving Jesus because he is worthy of devotion?

7. In the personal Bible study, you were asked to take a stab at writing out how Philip might have explained the good news of Jesus to the Ethiopian eunuch from Isaiah 53. Would any of you be willing to share what you wrote or take a stab at it if you didn't write something?

8. In Acts 8, we see Philip share the gospel of Jesus with despised outsiders and unwanted outcasts in his day. Of course, there are despised outsiders and unwanted outcasts in our day as well. What do you think it takes for us to overcome our prejudice, arrogance, or apathy so that we are willing to share the gospel with these outsiders and outcasts? What do we have that Philip had?

It can be difficult for us to admit, even to ourselves, that there are categories of people we avoid, dislike, or even despise. Let's pray that we would have the eyes to recognize our blind spots in regard to our own prejudices and ask the Lord for humility and grace to grow in love for all people.

Lesson 7

Discussion Questions

God's Chosen Instrument

ACTS 9:1–31

1. What stood out to you as you read this story of Saul's experience on the road to Damascus, whether you were hearing it for the first time or rereading a well-known passage?

2. Imagine yourself as Ananias. What might you have thought or felt when the Lord told you to go lay hands on Saul? What would it have been like for the other believers in Damascus to hear about Saul's conversion? (Consider that some of them may have known Stephen or had loved ones who were persecuted and killed in Jerusalem.)

3. If you were a believer in Saul's day, how do you think you might have felt about welcoming him into your church? What do you think it was like for Saul to have relationships with believers he had persecuted? What would both sides have needed for those relationships to flourish?

4. Read Galatians 1:11–16 together. What are some implications of the fact that God chose Paul to preach Christ among the Gentiles before he was even born? What does this tell us

about God's sovereignty over salvation and his providence in our lives?

5. Nancy said that when a person is saved, "it is always supernatural, though it might appear to be quite ordinary. It doesn't have to be sensational or emotional to be supernatural. Some people can tell you the moment when everything changed, and they became clear on who Jesus is. Others can't tell you exactly when it happened. But that doesn't mean it didn't." How does this encourage you or challenge you in your understanding of conversion?

6. Are there some members of this group who would be willing to share about their own conversion? How did they go from being spiritually dead to spiritually alive?

Before we pray, would anyone like to share the names of particular people you want us to ask God to supernaturally save? Let's pray together for the salvation of those people.

Lesson 8

Discussion Questions

What God Has Made Clean

ACTS 9:32–11:18

1. To really understand what transpired in this lesson, it helps to make sure we're clear on the Old Testament background for it. What was God's purpose in setting apart the Israelites to be his "treasured possession" from among the nations and giving them the holiness laws in Leviticus? How did the Jews misuse or misunderstand this?

2. Though we do not live under the Mosaic law, we have the same calling to be holy. What does it mean for Christians to pursue holiness? How can we avoid the errors of the first-century Jews?

3. Why do you think it requires divine revelation—repeated three times—for Peter to change how he sees the consumption of unclean animals?

4. Why is Peter's vision a necessary step in the fulfillment of Jesus's commission in Acts 1:8 ("You will be my witnesses in Jerusalem and in all Judea and Samaria, and to the end of the earth")?

5. Peter concludes by asking, "Who was I that I could stand in God's way?" (Acts 11:17). How might we "stand in God's way" of welcoming people into Christ's church today?

6. Acts 11:18 celebrates that God has granted the Gentiles "repentance that leads to life." How would you define *repentance*? In what ways does it lead to life?

7. Would anyone in the group be willing to share a personal experience of repentance leading to life?

Let's pray, asking God to grant us ongoing repentance that leads to life.

Lesson 9

Discussion Questions

The Hand of the Lord Was with Them

ACTS 11:19–12:25

1. When we think or speak about "the hand of the Lord" being on someone, what do you think we usually mean? Is that what we see in this passage?

2. Sometimes God works directly, but more often he works through means. Through what means do we see the hand of the Lord working in this passage?

3. This account of the Gentiles' sending relief to their sisters and brothers in Judea comes immediately after the story of Peter's experience in Caesarea. What do you think it would have been like for the Jewish Christians in Judea to receive a financial gift from the Gentile Christians in Antioch?

4. In 12:1, we read about Herod killing the apostle James. This is the first we've heard of James since the twelve apostles were together at Pentecost, which was about ten years earlier. What do you think James has been doing for those ten years? How do you think his murder would have impacted the believers in Jerusalem? (Acts 6:2–4 may give us a clue.)

5. The believers who have been praying for Peter's release don't believe it's him when he comes to the door. In what ways can you relate to this? Why do you think we struggle to believe that God will really answer our prayers?

6. We sometimes wonder why God chooses to heal or deliver some from harm, but not others. What scriptural truths can we lean into when we are troubled by questions like this?

7. Read together Acts 12:23–24. In light of all the events of chapter 12, how do these two verses give us perspective when it seems that evil is winning?

Let's close by asking God for the faith to trust him when we don't get what we are praying for, and when it seems like evil is winning in this world and in the lives of those we love.

Lesson 10

Discussion Questions

All That God Had Done with Them

ACTS 13:1–14:28

1. Have you ever expressed appreciation to someone for her ministry, and her response was, "Oh, it wasn't me, it was the Lord"—or have you said something similar yourself when recognized or thanked? What are the pros and cons of this type of response? What are some other ways we could respond?

2. Nancy said that Barnabas and Saul set off to fulfill a divine plan using human strategy. How would you describe the divine plan? And what elements are likely part of their human strategy?

3. At the first stop on their first missionary journey in Salamis, the Roman proconsul believes the gospel, and a Jewish magician experiences divine judgment. How do you think this would have impacted both Jews and Gentiles in this city? (Note especially what Paul says to Elymas in 13:10.)

4. How do we see both divine election and human response at work in Acts 13:48–52?

5. While we should always be prepared and take the opportunities God gives us to present Christ, we don't have to feel like failures when someone responds with apathy, indignation, or outright rejection. It's simply not all up to us. How does this encourage or challenge you as you think about sharing the gospel?

6. How is Paul's "sermon" to the Gentiles in Lystra (14:8–18) different from his sermon to the Jews and God-fearing Gentiles in Antioch in Pisidia (Acts 13:16–41)? How does this challenge you as you think about sharing Christ in different situations with different types of people?

7. Nancy said, "So often people think that if God will just do a miracle, then people will believe. But miracles don't always lead to genuine faith. They can lead to complete confusion." Why are miracles inadequate? What has God given us that leads to genuine faith?

8. How do we see both the Holy Spirit at work and humans working in this section of Acts? What implications does this have for our own ministry efforts?

Let's close by thanking God for his willingness to work in and through us, and by offering ourselves to him to be used for his purposes in the world.

Lesson 11

Discussion Questions

Saved through the Grace of the Lord Jesus

ACTS 15:1–16:5

1. In what way(s) does the disagreement regarding requiring Gentiles to become Jews before becoming Christians threaten the spread of the gospel?

2. Peter says in 15:11, "But we believe *we* will be saved through the grace of the Lord Jesus just as *they* will." Notice that even though they are discussing how Gentiles will be saved, he doesn't say, "But we believe *they* will be saved through the grace of the Lord Jesus just as *we* will." Why might that wording make a difference?

3. How are the Jewish and Gentile believers in the Antioch church encouraged and strengthened by the contingent from the Jerusalem church?

4. What does Colossians 4:10 (written many years after the events of Acts 15) reveal about the dispute between Paul, Mark, and Barnabas? How does that encourage you regarding church conflict you have experienced in the past or are experiencing in the present?

5. Timothy willingly submits to circumcision for the sake of helping Jews hear the gospel. Why do we bristle at the idea

of giving up our freedoms for the cause of the gospel? What are some examples today of freedoms that believers can enjoy, but might be wise to sacrifice for the sake of loving others and enabling them to hear the gospel?

6. In Acts 15:32; 15:41; and 16:5, we read that the churches are being strengthened, even though they're dealing with conflict. In what ways do you think working through conflict constructively can strengthen churches?

7. In this passage we covered a dispute about salvation requirements for Gentiles, a disagreement about ministry staffing, and a decision about how a disciple uses his or her freedom. What priorities guide how the early church works through each of these issues?

8. If you have been in the church for any length of time, you have likely experienced conflict. Church conflict often creates its own kind of hurt that can be hard to overcome. What do you think it looks like to walk through church conflict "in a manner worthy of the calling to which you have been called, with all humility and gentleness, with patience, bearing with one another in love, eager to maintain the unity of the Spirit in the bond of peace," as Ephesians 4:1–3 describes?

Let's close by asking God to give us the wisdom and the will to lay down our freedoms for the cause of the gospel. Let's also ask him for the wisdom and grace to navigate conflict in the church in a way that will bring him great glory and bless the church.

Lesson 12

Discussion Questions

There Is Another King, Jesus

ACTS 16:6–17:9

1. Have you ever made ministry plans that you were sure God would bless but then been prevented from carrying them out? How does this account of the Spirit's forbidding Paul and Silas's ministry plans help you think about your own thwarted ministry plans?

2. We might wish that God would give us visions that tell us exactly what to do, like he gave Paul. But how does God provide us with the guidance we need for ministry decisions?

3. Nancy proposed the possibility that Paul and Silas were singing Psalm 119, specifically vv. 61–62, while suffering in prison. What other psalms do you think would have been helpful in their circumstances? Are there certain psalms you find comforting to read or sing when you are suffering? What do you think it would have been like for the other prisoners and the jailer to hear their singing?

4. Have you ever experienced what seemed like supernatural joy or peace in the worst of circumstances? Or have you known

someone else who did? What is the effect of seeing someone demonstrate steadfast faith in Christ while suffering?

5. Nancy suggested that when the jailer asked "Sirs, what must I do to be saved?" he may not have been seeking spiritual salvation. If that is the case, in what way did he get much more than he even knew to ask for?

6. The mob in Thessalonica accused Paul and Silas of turning the world upside down. Think about what it was like to live under the kingdom of Rome and Caesar. In what ways did Paul and Silas's message of the kingdom of Jesus truly "turn the world upside down"? (For insights about Jesus's kingdom, consider reading Matt. 5:1–12; Luke 9:46–48; Luke 18:17, 24; John 18:36.)

7. How has the gospel of Jesus Christ continued to turn the world upside down in the two thousand years since Paul and Silas preached? What values does the kingdom of God proclaim that are the opposite of what our society values today? How does the kingdom of God challenge your own priorities and values?

Let's close by praying for God's kingdom to come in all of its "upside down" power to our world, our country, our city, our church, our families, and in our own lives.

Lesson 13

Discussion Questions

I Have Many in This City Who Are My People

ACTS 17:10–18:22

1. The Jews in Berea are "examining the Scriptures daily" (17:11) to see if what Paul is saying is so. We might instinctively imagine them in their homes reading their Bibles. But people don't have personal copies of the Old Testament Scriptures at this point. So what do you imagine this "examining" looked and sounded like?

2. What do you think it means that Paul's "spirit was provoked within him" (17:16) when he saw all the idols in Athens? Have you ever had a similar experience?

3. How is Paul's presentation of the gospel in Acts 17 dramatically different from what we've heard from him before? How does this challenge or instruct us as we present the gospel to various people?

4. In 17:26–27, Paul says, "And he made from one man every nation of mankind to live on all the face of the earth, having determined allotted periods and the boundaries of their dwelling place, that they should seek God, and perhaps feel their way toward him and find him. Yet he is actually not far from

each one of us." What does this reveal about God's sovereignty over people and people groups? How can this truth help you as you think about people you know and love who are outside of Christ?

5. In 17:34 we read that those who believe include "Dionysius the Areopagite and a woman named Damaris." Why do you think Luke may have included this detail?

6. Paul seems to have experienced some fear about taking the gospel to the pagan Gentiles in Corinth. Does that surprise you? Disappoint you? Encourage you? Why?

7. When we see the evil and idolatry of our day, some of us might be tempted to ignore, withdraw, or condemn. Others might be ready to thoughtfully engage, recognizing that God has many who are his people and need to hear the word of Christ. Which of these positions comes most naturally to you? What might need to change in order for you to engage with those around you who don't know Christ and may have social, sexual, and/ or political commitments that are offensive to you?

Let's close by asking God to give us the wisdom and courage to engage thoughtfully and helpfully with the world around us, for the cause of Christ and out of love for Christ.

Lesson 14

Discussion Questions

The Word Continued to Increase
and Prevail Mightily

ACTS 18:23–20:38

1. What do you think about the idea of being shaped by words? What are some specific words that have significantly shaped you?

2. What encourages or challenges you in the account of Priscilla, Aquila, and Apollos?

3. What do you think it means that the word of the Lord increased (Acts 6:7; 12:24)? And what do you think it means that the word of the Lord prevailed (19:20)?

4. When the new believers in Ephesus burn their magic books, which are worth a great deal of money, they demonstrate costly obedience and sanctification. We don't read that Paul admonished them to do this, but that they come voluntarily, "confessing and divulging their practices" (19:18). What does this scene tell us about their repentance?

5. What kinds of costly ways might new believers today need to live out repentance and sanctification? How might those

who have followed Jesus a long time still need to demonstrate costly obedience and sanctification?

6. Nancy described the word in Ephesus as a "dangerous" word. In what ways, or to what, was the word of God dangerous?

7. Why do you think Luke seems to want us to see the fellowship of believers around the table and the preaching of the word as more significant than the miracle of raising a person from the dead?

8. Paul said goodbye to the Ephesian elders with a clear conscience that he had declared to them "the whole counsel of God," (20:27). Other translations speak of the whole "will" (NIV), "purpose" (NASB), or "plan" (CSB) of God. So perhaps we could say that Paul taught them everything they needed to know to live out the Christian life. If you knew you were having your last conversation with someone you love and wanted to tell them what they most need to know to live out the Christian life going forward, what kinds of things would you say?

Let's close by asking God to use his word to make a deep and lasting impression in our lives, shaping us into the image of Christ.

Lesson 15

Discussion Questions

Paul Resolved in His Spirit to Go to Jerusalem

ACTS 21:1–23:30

1. Do you agree that personal safety has become an accepted idol in our day—that it is more important to us than advancing the gospel of Jesus Christ? Why or why not?

2. What message are we getting from the book of Acts about personal safety? Can you think of other places in the New Testament where Paul speaks about danger or risking life for the cause of the gospel?

3. Paul knows that he will face suffering in Jerusalem. Why is he so determined to go there anyway? What does he hope this trip will accomplish?

4. Why do you think Paul is willing to submit to an Old Testament purification ritual and to pay the cost for four men under a Nazirite vow?

5. After Paul was nearly torn to pieces by the Jewish mob, "the Lord stood by him" and assured him that he would "testify also in Rome" (23:11). How would that have made a difference to Paul over the coming years he spent in custody?

6. Has there been a low time in your life when you sensed "the Lord stood by" you? How have you experienced Jesus's comfort and presence in the midst of suffering?

7. Nancy said, "We have an incredible impulse toward self-preservation and very little inclination toward self-denial. It makes us wonder if it is really possible that we could deny ourselves, take up our cross, and follow Jesus." What do you think it takes for people like you and me to overcome self-preservation and to embrace self-denial and even danger? How could we help each other do this more?

Let's close by asking God to give us the grace and wisdom to embrace self-denial and take appropriate risks for the sake of the gospel.

Lesson 16

Discussion Questions

I Always Take Pains to Have a Clear
Conscience toward God and Man

ACTS 24:1–26:32

1. Is it really possible to be self-aware about our pervasive sinfulness, especially at the level of inner thoughts and motives, and yet have a clear conscience? Why or why not?

2. What are some ways we try to deal with a sullied conscience? What is the good news of the gospel for those of us with a sullied conscience?

3. Throughout Acts, and again here, the message of the apostles has been summarized as the resurrection from or of the dead (4:2; 17:32; 23:6; 24:21). Hopefully we've gotten clear on the meaning of this phrase, but just in case, what do the apostles mean when they say that their message or hope is the resurrection of the dead?

4. In 24:25 we're told that Paul reasons with Felix about righteousness, self-control, and the coming judgment. Why do you think each of these things might have caused Felix to respond with alarm? (A few notes that might be helpful: Paul would have written his letter to the Romans by this point, so

you might consider his teaching on righteousness in Rom. 3:10–12, 21–26. Felix was known to be a cruel tyrant. According to Josephus, Felix seduced and lured Drusilla away from her first husband to make her his third wife.)

5. Read Romans 12:14–13:7, which Paul has already written by the time he stands before Felix, Festus, and Agrippa. How do you see Paul living out his own instructions? How does his example challenge you as you evaluate your attitudes and actions toward governing authorities?

6. In her introduction, Nancy asked, "What does it mean to be saved?" In Acts 26:16–23, Paul articulates what it means to be saved. As we approach the end of this study, how has your understanding of salvation changed or developed? What have you grown to appreciate about God's outworking of his salvation plan?

Let's close by thanking God for making it possible to live with a clear conscience because of the sacrifice of Jesus, and for our increasing grasp of what it means that we have been saved, are being saved, and will be saved.

Lesson 17

Discussion Questions

It Will Be Exactly as I Have Been Told

ACTS 27:1–28:31

1. We could title Acts 27–28 "God's Power to Save." How do we see God's power to save in these chapters?

2. In what ways is Paul's whole life a testimony to God's power to save?

3. Paul has faith in God that the safe passage of all on the ship to Rome will be exactly as he has been told. What are some promises in the Bible that you can take hold of, having full confidence that it will be exactly as you have been told?

4. What are some Bible verses that people take hold of as "promises," but that aren't really promises we can claim? What is the danger of clinging to these verses as promises?

5. Throughout the book of Acts, opposition to the gospel has come from many sources, both human and supernatural. List as many sources as you can remember: who has been against the gospel? What has this book shown us about opposition to the gospel?

6. Do you think Acts ends on a victorious note? Why or why not?

7. Back in the introduction, we looked at several possible titles for this book. Having now worked your way through Acts, in what way do you see each of these as a possibility?

- The Acts of the Apostles
- The Acts of the Holy Spirit
- The Acts of the Preached Word
- The Acts of the Enthroned Lord Jesus

8. When Luke began writing the first of his two-book series, the Gospel of Luke, he wrote, "It seemed good to me also, having followed all things closely for some time past, to write an orderly account for you, most excellent Theophilus, that you may have certainty concerning the things you have been taught" (Luke 1:3–4). What can you take away with certainty from the things you have seen in Acts?

9. How will your certainty about these truths impact the way you live?

Let's close by asking the Spirit who came at Pentecost to indwell his people, and who dwells in us even now, to implant these truths from Acts deep in our souls. Let's ask him to increase our confidence in God's salvation and expand our love for people, from those around us to those who are at the ends of the earth.

Resources to Go Deeper in Your Study of Acts

Saved: Experiencing the Promise of the Book of Acts

Saved Video Study (DVD or Download)

Saved Personal Bible Study (Paperback or Printable PDF)

Saved Leader's Guide (Paperback or Printable PDF)

ESV Scripture Journal: Acts (Saved Edition)

For more information, visit **crossway.org**.